Pray Like Jesus

An Exploration In Prayer

John R. Brokhoff

CSS Publishing Company, Inc.
Lima, Ohio

PRAY LIKE JESUS

Copyright © 1994 by
The CSS Publishing Company, Inc.
Lima, Ohio

Library of Congress Cataloging-in-Publication Data
Brokhoff, John R., 1913-
    Pray like Jesus : for personal reflection and group discussion / John R. Brokhoff.
        p.   cm.
    ISBN 0-7880-0105-1
1. Prayer. 2. Jesus Christ—Prayers. 3. Prayer—Biblical teaching. I. Title
BV210.2.B73   1994
248.3'2—dc   94-227
                                                                                CIP

This book is available in the following formats, listed by ISBN:
0-7880-0105-1 Book
0-7880-0106-X IBM (3 1/2 and 5 1/4) computer disk
0-7880-0107-8 IBM book and disk package
0-7880-0108-6 Macintosh computer disk
0-7880-0109-4 Macintosh book and disk package

PRINTED IN U.S.A.

*To all who prayed for my recovery
from brain surgery following a
car accident in 1991 including
Dr. Thomas Edison Farmer
and Members of St. Paul United Methodist
Church in Largo, Florida.*

Table Of Contents

In The School
Of Prayer

Prayer is not limited to any one religion. No religion has a monopoly on prayer. All peoples of all religions for all ages pray to whatever god they worship. All religions have at least one thing in common — they pray! Christians, therefore, have no monopoly on praying. Jesus assumed that everyone prays. In the Sermon on the Plain, Jesus said, "When you pray . . ." (Luke 11:2). He did not say "if" you pray, or "should" you pray, or "in case" you pray, but "when" you pray.

But, do all people pray? To what extent is prayer practiced in America? A few years ago there was a Gallup poll of 1,500 people in and out of the church. The poll revealed that 87 percent said they prayed. They "said" they prayed, but did they? Perhaps the percentage was high because there was no indication of the frequency of their prayers.

In 1992, a Protestant denomination made a study of the prayer habits of its members. The study indicated that 40 percent said grace before meals daily, 6 percent weekly, and 3 percent monthly. As for personal prayers, 53 percent said they prayed daily, 7 percent weekly, and 17 percent monthly. According to this study, roughly half of the church members prayed daily.

But, all people should pray. In Conyers, Georgia, 20,000 people gather to see and hear a miraculous revelation of the Virgin Mary. The report is that Mary's message was "America, pick up your rosary. *Kneel down and pray.*" We may not feel the need of a rosary, but we should heed the message, "Kneel down and pray, America." Our country is a sick society resulting from moral corruption, AIDS, drug and alcohol abuse, and the disintegration of the family. America is standing in the need of prayer. Only God through prayer can cure our sickness.

Lord, Teach Us To Pray (Luke 11:1)

What We Want To Learn

What do we want Jesus to teach us? The Disciples said, "Lord, teach us to *pray.*" This is the one and only time the Disciples asked Jesus to teach them. They did not ask him to teach them how to love, or how to live, or how to forgive, or how to serve. No, they needed a lesson on prayer.

Prayer — what is that? Prayer is conversation with God. In prayer we do not talk *to* God but *with* God. When we talk with people, we talk on a horizontal basis, person to person on the same level. When we talk with God, there is a perpendicular dimension. Since this is true, what shall we say to God and how shall we say it? What words shall we use? What attitude should we have? Here I am — a lost and miserable sinner in the very presence of a holy, righteous, omnipotent God of glory. What a privilege and honor it is just to talk with God!

Why do we pray? Why is prayer so very important? Consider these answers:

1. To experience God's presence — to have fellowship with him.

2. To learn God's will for our lives.

3. To get strength to do God's will.

4. To receive answers to our petitions.

5. To express our thanks and praise for his goodness and mercy.

Prayer Can Be Learned *"Teach* Us To Pray"

Evelyn Underhill once wrote: "Teaching about prayer is the teaching most needed at the moment." Prayer can be

8

taught because it is not a natural trait. It is not instinctive. We must learn to pray. The New Testament refers to us as "babes in Christ." New-born babies cannot talk, not even a syllable. Parents patiently teach the child to say its first word "Momma" or "Daddy."

Learning to pray is a lifelong process. It begins when parents teach the simple, easy prayers such as "Now I lay me down to sleep" or a table prayer as "God is great and God is good." As the years come, our prayers should increase in maturity as we learn more and more of God's nature. Life's experiences of sorrow, tragedy, defeat, and even joyful experiences teach us to improve our prayers. If you think you do not know how to pray, cheer up because you can still learn!

Who Is Able To Teach Us?   *"Lord,* Teach Us ..."

The Disciples knew to whom to go to get instruction in prayer. They saw and heard him pray and they wanted to learn how to pray like him. In the hymn, "Go to Dark Gethsemane," one of the stanzas closes: "Learn of Jesus Christ to pray."

Jesus never said he did not know how to pray. His prayer life was based on his relationship with his Father-God. No human since the creation of humanity was as close to God as Jesus was. He said, "The Father and I are one" (John 10:30), "I can do nothing on my own" (John 5:30), and "Believe me that I am in the Father and the Father in me" (John 14:11). This oneness with the Father enabled him to know all about prayer because he knew all about God.

Who Needs To Learn To Pray?   "Lord, Teach *Us* ..."

"Us" — who is us? Are we included? Do we need to learn to pray? The Disciples are among the "us." They saw in Jesus and his prayer life what prayer can do. They came to Jesus with their request because they admitted they did not know how to pray. Paul was also included in the "us." In Romans 8:26 Paul wrote, "We do not know how to pray as we ought." Indeed, he prayed but not "as we ought." This seems to be the only thing connected with the Gospel that Paul did not know how to do. He knew how to write letters that the Christian world is still reading. He knew how to explain the meaning of the Gospel. He knew how to attack false prophets of his day and to defend the Gospel. He knew how to plant churches all over the Graeco-Roman world. Yet, he did not know how to pray as he ought. So, he would say, "Lord, teach us to pray."

In fact the author of this book on prayer must confess that he does not know how to pray as he ought. In spite of the fact that he has been praying ever since his mother taught him as a little boy to say the Lord's Prayer; in spite of the fact that as a pastor for over 50 years he has been leading individuals and congregations in prayer; in spite of the fact that he recently read a couple dozen books on prayer, he still does not feel as though he knows how to pray as he ought. By writing this book and teaching the course, "Pray like Jesus," he hopes to learn with you more about prayer. Both reader and author will work together in learning how to pray.

Are you included in the "us"? Do you need to go to Jesus along with the Disciples and ask Jesus for lessons? To answer, ask yourself these questions:

1. When you pray, do you feel you are talking to yourself?
2. Are your words seemingly bouncing back from the ceiling?
3. Has prayer become a meaningless habit?
4. Are you getting no answers?
5. Do you pray only when in a crisis?
6. Are you any different because you prayed?

Supplemental Reading On Prayer

John Baillie, *A Diary of Private Prayer*
Oswald Chambers, *My Utmost for the Highest*

Harry Emerson Fosdick, *The Meaning of Prayer*
Richard C. Foster, *Prayer*
Thomas R. Kelly, *A Testament of Devotion*
Thomas A. Kempis, *The Imitation of Christ*
Brother Lawrence, *The Practice of the Presence of God*
Andrew Murray, *With Christ in the School of Prayer*
Lance Webb, *The Art of Personal Prayer*

A Personal Project

For the 13 weeks of this course, keep a journal of your spiritual journey in prayer to enable you to measure your growth in prayer. At the end of each day, write about your experiences in prayer. Any results? Any improvements in your prayers? Perhaps you would like to write a prayer for each day.

Possible Uses Of This Book

Personal use. The book can be studied by one who feels the need to improve one's prayers. At the end of each chapter, there are questions for private reflection.

Group use. Classes in the church school can use this course for a quarter of the year — 13 sessions for 13 Sundays. Also, the book can be used as an elective in the Sunday church school, or as a course in a weekday Interdenominational School of Religion. Questions for group discussion are at the close of each chapter.

Church Use. The course of prayer can be offered in many ways throughout the congregation. The circles of women's societies or the men's groups could use it for monthly programs. During the Lenten season the book, chapter by chapter, could be used in place of the sermon time.

1

Jesus
The Pray-er

Jesus is often called our teacher, leader, redeemer but rarely, if ever, is he referred to as our pray-er. Yet, Jesus was the greatest pray-er the world has ever known. Because he was a man of God, he was also a man of prayer. No person ever prayed like he did. For him prayer was as natural and necessary as breathing. Through prayer he learned who he was and what his purpose in life was. Prayer was his way of staying in communion with his Father who guided him and empowered him to do God's will. If we are going to pray like Jesus, we need to review the prayer life of Jesus. It would be well if you, the reader, had a Bible to read the passages in our study.

When Jesus Prayed

We begin the study of Jesus' prayer life with the start of his ministry which occurred at his baptism by John the Baptist in the river Jordan. According to Luke his baptism was a prayer experience: "When Jesus also had been baptized and was praying." *Read* Luke 3:21. His baptism was his ordination to be the Messiah. At this time he received the Holy Spirit and heard God's acceptance and approval as God's Son.

Though Matthew, Mark, and Luke do not refer specifically to Jesus' praying during his temptation while he was in the wilderness for 40 days, it is inconceivable that prayer was not a vital part of his experience. At his baptism he realized who he was and what his work was to be, but how was he going to do it? Satan suggested three different ways, but Jesus turned them down as not being in harmony with Scripture.

To make the right choice of method, he must have prayed for guidance. *Read* Matthew 4:1-11.

Having made the right choice of a method to be the Messiah, Jesus needed disciples. Who should they be? Of the thousands he knew, who was best qualified to be the future leaders of the church? In an all-night prayer Jesus asked his Father for guidance in making the choice. "He spent the night in prayer to God. And when the day came, he called his disciples." *Read* Luke 6:12-13.

A healthy soul is a thankful soul. Being a healthy soul, Jesus continually thanked God. In thanking God, he revealed his dependence on God and acknowledged the goodness of God as the giver of everything good. At one time he thanked his Father for revealing the truth to "infants," his Disciples. "I thank you, Father, ... because you have hidden these things from the wise and the intelligent and revealed them to infants." *Read* Matthew 11:25. Before feeding the 4,000 and 5,000, Jesus said grace before the meal: "After giving thanks he broke them and gave them to his Disciples to distribute." *Read* Mark 8:6.

Jesus began the day by praying. He was following Psalm 5:3 — "O Lord, in the morning you hear my voice; in the morning I plead my case to you." Apparently, Jesus found the morning a good time to pray, for morning prayer sets the tone for the whole day. "In the morning while it was still very dark ... and there he prayed." *Read* Mark 1:35.

Before starting out for Jerusalem for the last time, Jesus needed to be sure that his ministry was acceptable to God. Before he went through the passion he had to know whether God approved. To get this approval, God repeats that Jesus is God's beloved Son. His purpose of going up the mountain was to pray. Jesus "went up on the mountain to pray." *Read* Luke 9:28-29.

Jesus now faces the crisis of his life. It is a matter of life and death. Shall he go to the cross? Shall he be obedient to his call received at his baptism? This takes him to the Garden of Gethsemane. There he struggles with his Father. He tells

14

his Disciples, "Sit here while I go over there and pray." *Read* Matthew 26:36-46.

From this review of the times Jesus prayed, we learn to pray when Jesus did. We need to pray when we face major experiences like baptism and Transfiguration. When we face serious decisions such as the choice of disciples, we want to pray for guidance. Many times, even daily, we will, if we pray like Jesus, thank God for his blessings. When we face a crisis of life or death, we will have our Gethsemane. At the hour of death we will turn our thoughts to God in prayer. The truth is, there is never a time when prayer is not appropriate.

What Jesus Prayed For

If we are going to pray like Jesus, we need to know the content of his prayers. He prayed for his closest friends such as Peter right before he was arrested. Jesus was concerned for the faith of his leader when the stress came. "I have prayed for you that your own faith may not fail." *Read* Luke 22:31-34.

The perfect love of Jesus was manifest in his prayer for those murdering him. His first word on the cross: "Father, forgive them ..." *Read* Luke 23:34. His last word on the cross was a prayer commending his soul into God's hands. What a way to die! It was the perfect end to a perfect life. *Read* Luke 23:46.

We can see the content of his prayers by looking at several of his prayers. Take a look, first, at the prayer he taught his Disciples. *Read* Matthew 6:9-13; Luke 11:1-4. It opens with praise and adoration. There follow three "Thy" petitions dealing with God's name, kingdom, and will. Four petitions deal with us: our food, forgiveness, temptation, and deliverance. This prayer is considered the perfect prayer.

A second prayer occurred in the Garden of Gethsemane. *Read* Matthew 26:36-46. In verse 36, Jesus goes for privacy and solitude. His petition is found in verse 38 — "Let this cup pass from me." His posture is described in verse 39 — he "threw himself on the ground." Submission to God's will occurs in verses 39 and 42 — "Yet not what I want but what you want." He prayed persistently — verse 44 — "Prayed for the third time." Moreover, he prayed so earnestly that "his sweat became like great drops of blood falling down on the ground." The author of Hebrews tells us that "Jesus offered up prayers and supplications with loud cries and tears" (5:7).

The entire chapter of John contains Jesus' high priestly prayer. In it he prayed for himself — "Glorify me that I may glorify you" — verses 1-8. Then he prayed for us, his future disciples.

To pray like Jesus, what will be the content of our prayers? There will be intercession for friends as well as enemies. Through prayer we will daily commit ourselves to God. In our Gethsemanes we will seek to know God's will for our lives. As in John 17, we will pray for all sorts and conditions of people.

We have been looking at what Jesus prayed for. It is important to note what he did *not* pray for. He never confessed sin nor asked for forgiveness. He asked his enemies, "Which of you convicts me of sin?" (John 8:46). Why would he pray for forgiveness when he was above all interested only in spiritual wealth? Thus, he never prayed for material benefits such as food, clothing, comfort, success or power.

How Jesus Prayed

How Jesus prayed can be seen in his teachings which he put into practice. First, he told us about the environment for prayer. *Read* Matthew 6:6. The environment consists of —
> Solitude — "Go into your room."
> Silence — "Shut the door."
> Secrecy — "Pray to your Father in secret."

There should be an economy of words. *Read* Matthew 6:7. "They think that they will be heard because of their many words. Your Father knows what you need before you ask him." Jesus warned us not to use vain repetitions.

16

In his prayers there were petitions. He taught, "Ask —
Search — Knock." *Read* Matthew 7:7. The Lord's Prayer, his
Gethsemane prayer, as well as his prayers on the cross con-
tained petitions. It is right, therefore, for us to ask what we
and others need.

Jesus taught that we should pray with forgiveness just as
he did when on the cross. *Read* Mark 11:25. "Whenever you
stand praying, forgive . . ." Pray also persistently. He taught
this in two parables: the friend at midnight asking for bread
(Luke 11:5-8), and the widow and the unjust judge (Luke
18:1-8).

When we pray we should be humble because who are we
in contrast to a holy God? Jesus taught this in the parable of
two men praying in the temple. *Read* Luke 18:9-14.

Jesus would have us pray with confidence even as he was
confident of God's answering our prayers. "If in my name
you ask me for anything, I will do it." *Read* John 14:13-14.

A Case Study

Luke 11:1-13

1. We do not know how to pray — v. 1 — "Teach us to
pray."
2. The content of prayer — vv. 2-4.
3. Persistence — prayer may not be answered immediately — vv. 5-8. "Because of his persistence he will get up and
give him whatever he needs." v. 8.
4. Encouraged to pray — v. 9 — "Ask — Search —
Knock."
5. Prayers will be answered — v. 10.
6. God gives only the good — vv. 11-13.

Personal Reflection/Group Discussion

1. Is it humanly possible to pray like Jesus?

2. Since God knows what we need even before we pray, why bother to pray?

3. To what extent does one's relationship with God affect one's prayers?

4. When facing a crisis, do you hesitate to ask for guidance in fear he will ask you to do something you do not want to do?

5. Since most of us do not know how to pray as we ought, how can we improve our prayers?

6. Does it matter what we pray for so long as we ask for it in Jesus' name?

"O Thou full of compassion, I commit and commend myself unto Thee in whom I am and live and know. Be Thou the goal of my pilgrimage and the rest by the way. Let me take refuge from the crowding turmoil of worldly thoughts beneath the shadow of Thy wings. And let my heart, this sea of restlessness, find peace in Thee, O God. Amen."

— St. Augustine

2
A Theology Of Prayer

Why do we pray? Is praying a talking to God or to self? What is our reason for thinking there is a God who bothers to listen to human prayers? Are we deluding ourselves by praying? What is our rationale for praying? How do we justify it? This leads to a consideration of a theology of prayer.

Biblical Basis For Prayer

Prayer is based upon the existence of God. If there is no God, we are talking to ourselves and wasting our time. The Bible, the record of God's self-revelation, assures us God truly exists. We enter into prayer with the conviction that God is real, a real person, the Father of our Lord Jesus Christ. He is not an abstract principle, nor an ideal, nor a figment of our imagination. He is as real as you and I are. As a real personality, he knows, he wills, he judges, he loves.

Is God real to you? Is he one you know only by hearsay? Is he only a part of your religious tradition? When I was a pastor in Charlotte, North Carolina, I had a physician who was a very faithful member. He rarely, if ever, missed a church service and attended various organizations. He was a member of the governing board of the congregation. Some years later I was invited back to preach and met his widow. She told me that a few months before he died of cancer, he had an experience with Christ. He was so very excited about this experience. She said it gave him so much joy and peace. I was happy to get the good news, but it made me wonder how for years he could have been such a faithful member and not known Christ. Where had I as his pastor failed him? It is quite possible that a church member can go through the externals of religion without knowing God.

If God is real, do we have a relationship with him? Our prayer life depends upon this relationship. Is it a relationship which enables us to call him Father? How does one get this relationship? It is established at the time of baptism when God accepts the person as his child, forgives sin, and bestows the Holy Spirit. Henceforth, a baptized person can approach Almighty God with full confidence that God allows the person to come into his presence to pray.

One time a Roman emperor was returning from a victorious battle. A platform was erected for his family to watch the victory parade. When the procession came near the viewing stand, the emperor's little son jumped down and squeezed through the crowd toward his father's chariot. One of the legionnaires picked him up and said, "You can't run out there. Don't you know who is in that chariot? That's the emperor. You cannot run out to him." The little guy laughed and said, "He may be your emperor, but he's my father!" Because God is our heavenly Father, we can go to him in prayer without fear of being turned away.

The Nature Of God

We pray to a real God, but what kind of a God is he? Our prayers depend upon the nature of God. He is a God of power, an omnipotent, almighty God. Jesus told his Disciples, "For God all things are possible" (Matthew 19:26). He is able to do all things. The Bible asks, "Is anything too hard for God?" We cannot ask anything of him that is beyond his ability to provide. He is able to help, to cure, and even to perform miracles in our behalf.

God is not only able but he is a loving God. As the Scriptures say, "God is love." Because of this love, he cares for us. He is concerned when we are in trouble. He wants to help us. Not only is he able but he is willing to help us. This God of love hears the prayers of his people. He always answers every prayer — "Ask and it will be given you" (Matthew 7:7). Every answer is good for us. A good, loving God would never send us anything that was not for our good. Thus, Paul wrote, "Let your requests be made known to God" (Philippians 4:6).

Because of the nature of our creation, God causes us to pray to him. We are God's creation. By his redemption we are children of God. When Adam was created, God breathed into Adam and he became a living soul. This living soul was made in the image of God. Therefore, a human has the capacity to have fellowship with God. As a result of our creation, we are incurably religious. If we did not have God, we would make our own gods as Aaron and the Israelites did in the wilderness. Like a homing pigeon instinctively flies home, so our spirits reach up to God. As a result all peoples everywhere since creation have prayed. St. Augustine rightly prayed, "Our souls are restless until they rest in Thee."

The Nature Of Prayer

To learn to pray like Jesus, we need to understand why we pray. Why do we pray? The purpose of prayer was excellently stated by Richard Foster: "To bring us into such a life of communion with the Father that, by the power of the Spirit, we are increasingly conformed to the image of the Son."

Prayer Is Petition

Though it is the lowest form of prayer, it is essential. Jesus commanded us to ask: "Ask, seek, knock." In the Lord's Prayer there are six petitions. James writes, "You do not have because you do not ask" (James 4:2). The weakness of this type of prayer is that if we need nothing, we will not pray. A pastor asked a little boy if he prayed every night. "No, sir, not every night, some nights I don't want anything." If prayer is restricted to asking, we make of God a cosmic Santa Claus. If your conversation with your parent was only when you wanted something, what kind of a relationship was that? Contrast this with another boy's prayer. He knelt at his mother's knee and offered his bedtime prayer. He spoke so softly his mother could not hear what he said. When he finished she asked him, "What did you ask for?" He answered, "I didn't ask for anything. I just told God that I loved him."

Prayer Is Fellowship

Prayer is the means of being in God's presence. We call it fellowship or communion. George MacDonald taught, "Communion with God is the one need of the soul beyond all other need: prayer is the beginning of that communion." Prayer is the glorious privilege of being one with God. In this type of prayer, there is no need for words. There is silence but also a sense of God's presence. In this way you can pray unceasingly as St. Paul urged us to do. It is living throughout the day in the presence of God, as Brother Lawrence did while working in the monastery's kitchen washing pots and pans. Oswald Chambers explained, "The point of prayer is not in order to get answers from God; prayer is perfect and complete oneness with God. Prayer is not getting things from God. Prayer is getting into perfect communion with God."

Prayer Is Communication

Prayer is conversation with God. It is a time not to talk *to* but *with* God. A child was softly saying her prayers one night. Her mother said, "I can't hear you, dear." "Wasn't talking to you," she firmly replied.

When we pray we talk with God as we talk to a father or to a friend. We bare our hearts and tell all. We seek his guidance. We want to know what his will is in a given situation and ask for strength to do it. This is what Jesus did in Gethsemane: "Not my will but yours be done."

If prayer is conversation, it therefore is a dialogue. Not only do we speak, but God speaks to us. Ever have that experience? To hear God speak may shock you. H. G. Wells tells of a troubled archbishop who went one night to the chapel to pray. He began as usual, "O God . . ." There came from the altar a strong voice replying, "Yes, what is it?" Next morning they found him sprawled on the altar steps. He had died of shock. For God to speak to us, he does not have to speak audibly. He speaks to us whenever the Word is read or heard.

Prayer Is A Way Of Living

Henry Nouwen in *The Practice Of The Presence Of God* explains, "Prayer is not saying prayers but a way of living in which all we do becomes prayer. We indeed are called not just to say prayers but to live a prayerful life. A prayerful life is a life in which all we do is done to the glory of God."

The way we live is reflected in our prayers. A person who lives only for him/herself prays in terms of petitions only. People who have concern for other people pray prayers of intercession asking God to bless them and fulfill their needs. The person who thinks of serving God says prayers of submission: "Your will be done."

A study of our prayers will reveal our faith in God, our goals and values that we hold dear, our concern for others, and the condition of our relationship with God. Our prayers reflect who we are — our thinking and our understanding of life.

Our Prayer Sins

Did you ever think you can sin by praying? James writes, "You ask and do not receive, because you ask wrongly" (James 4:3). If we pray amiss, we are sinning. How could this be?

First, we can use prayer for human achievement rather than seeing prayer as a product of grace. We count the hours spent in prayer. We repeat prayers hundreds of time. We emphasize our excellent vocalization of prayer by the use of eloquence. In these ways, we think we can overcome God's reluctance to answer our prayers. If we get an answer, we consider it a reward for the quantity and quality of our prayers. This is the sin of works righteousness.

Second, we may use prayer as an excuse for doing nothing about what we pray for. We expect God to do for us what we can or should do for ourselves. A wealthy man prided himself on being a devout and good man. He led family prayers every morning. He prayed especially for an aged couple who lived near his estate. They were both poor and ill. The rich man's nine-year-old son was in the prayer group one Sunday morning. He asked his father if he had stopped to see the old couple for whom he prayed. When the father said he did not, the lad said, "Dad, I wish I had your money." When his father asked why, his son answered, "Because I could answer your prayers." To pray for others when we could help is a cop-out. God often answers our prayers by using us.

Third, we often see the sign or hear the words, "Prayer Changes Things." No, prayer does not change things but changes people. Then people change things. Prayer does not change inanimate things. God works through people. Prayer does not change even God. By prayer we do not get in tune with God but God gets in tune with us. We do not try to get God's will to bend to us but we bend our wills to God's.

Getting Through To God

Effective pray-ers get through to God. How can we do this? God is the invisible and incomprehensible one. He is the totally other. No human can see God, stand in his presence, or understand him. Prayer is our means of getting through to almighty God through the Trinity. We address our prayers to God the Father. To get to the Father, we go through the Son, our Mediator. He takes our petitions to his Father and pleads on our behalf. In taking our prayers to Jesus, we are led by the Holy Spirit who teaches us what and how to pray.

Reflection/Discussion

1. If God is love and wants us to have only good things, why pray?

2. How would you respond to one who claims prayer is only wishful thinking?

3. Why pray in a world of unchangeable natural laws?

4. Explain: "What you are is how you pray."

5. How can God become real to a person?

6. Does God expect us to cooperate with him in answering prayer?

"Create in me a clean heart, O God, and renew a right spirit within me. Cast me not away from Thy presence and take not Thy Holy Spirit from me. Restore unto me the joy of Thy salvation and uphold me with Thy free Spirit."

— Psalm 51:10-12

3

Prayers In
The Bible

How did the people in the Bible pray? In one Bible supplementary helps list 85 prayers. Since the writers and characters of the Bible were close to God, their prayers should be able to teach us how to improve our prayers. How did they approach God? What language did they use? Were their prayers answered? Are there any lessons to be learned from their prayers? Let us look at some of these prayers.

Jacob The Wrestler — Genesis 32:22-32

Jacob's prayer reminds us that prayer can be a struggle. Think of it as a wrestling match. As you have probably seen a wrestling match on TV, you know it can be very rough: bodies thrown down, limbs twisted with excruciating pain. Prayer is not always quiet and peaceful. It can be a bloody sweat as it was for Jesus in Gethsemane. Prayer can writhe your soul as you wrestle with God.

Before we can understand this prayer of Jacob, we need to recall the background and context of the prayer. Jacob had a bad record with his twin brother, Esau. He persuaded Esau to sell him his birthright for a dish of food at a time when Esau was famished. Jacob took unfair advantage of his brother and gained the rights of a first-born son. Esau resented this for years (Genesis 25:29-34). When his father Isaac was about to die, Jacob with the help of his mother, camouflaged himself to look and smell like Esau to get his father's blessing (Genesis 27:30-38). This enraged Esau to the point that he planned to murder Jacob. To protect him, his mother sent him away to his uncle Laban (Genesis 27:41-45). In the 14 years Jacob worked for Laban, he gained two wives and a bundle of livestock. He decided to return to his ancestral home, but on the way he learned that Esau with 400 armed men was coming to meet him. To appease Esau and to win his favor, he sent gifts ahead (Genesis 32:13-21).

As Esau drew nearer, the tension in Jacob grew more intense. He sent his wives and children across the Jabbok river and he stayed on the other side. There he was all alone and he began to pray. It was portrayed as wrestling with a "man." He persists in his struggle saying, "I will not let you go, unless you bless me" (v. 26). The "man" asked Jacob for his name and then changed it to "Israel" (v. 28). Jacob asked his name, but the request was refused. But his prayer was answered, "And there he blessed him" (v. 29). His prayer was further answered when he found that Esau had forgiven and accepted him. Jacob said to Esau, "Truly to see your face is like seeing the face of God — since you have received me with such favor" (33:10).

Who was the "man"? He was God wrestling like a man. This "man" identified himself, "You have striven with God" (v. 28). Jacob called the wrestling place "Peniel, for I have seen God face to face" (v. 30).

Jacob was never the same man after this prayer. He was struck on his hip so that it was out of joint. Thereafter, Jacob walked with a limp (v. 31).

What Can We Learn From Jacob's Prayer?

1. Prayer can be a struggle between God's and our wills.
2. Like Jacob, our past can catch up with us. In 1993 a woman, after 23 years hiding from the FBI because she participated in a bank robbery in which a policeman was killed, surrendered herself and went to prison.
3. Jacob teaches us persistence in our prayers. He prayed all night and refused to let God go until he blessed him.

4. Jacob did his part in answering his own prayer by sending gifts to Esau to win his favor. God expects us to cooperate with him in answering our prayers.

5. Prayers are answered. Jacob was blessed. Esau's revenge dissolved into grace.

6. Prayer leaves an impression. Jacob went away limping. We kneel how weak; we rise how strong!

Moses The Intercessor — Exodus 32:30-35

In his prayer, Moses proves he is an intercessor, praying for his people and offering his life to make atonement for their great sin. A second account of his intercession may be found in Deuteronomy 9:15-21, 25-29.

Take a look at the background of Moses' prayer. Why did he offer this prayer? Moses was on the top of Mt. Sinai 40 days receiving the covenant containing the Decalogue (32:1). He stayed so long that the people at the foot of the mountain thought he either died or deserted them. They come to Aaron, their high priest, and demand he make another god for them (32:1). With the gold jewelry offered by the people, Aaron fashioned a calf of gold (32:2-4). An altar was put in front of the statue, and the people held a religious festival with sacrifices, food, and drink (32:5-6). God knows of their sin and sends Moses down the mountain. God is determined to destroy the people (32:10). After the calf was constructed, Aaron assured the people they did the right thing by giving them twice the big lie: "These are your gods, O Israel, who brought you up out of the land of Egypt" (vv. 4, 8).

In the light of this situation, Moses takes it to the Lord in prayer. First, he tells the people they have committed "a great sin" (v. 30). Then he turns to God and confesses on the people's behalf that they committed "a great sin" (v. 31). That "great sin," of course, was their making their own god of gold. They slipped back to the pagan gods of Egypt. Moses pleads for their forgiveness. To get it Moses offers to sacrifice himself as an offering to placate the wrath of God. Moses' prayer is answered. Forgiveness is granted and Moses is ordered to continue leading the Israelites to the Promised Land (v. 34). Nevertheless, punishment is forthcoming.

What Can We Learn From Moses' Prayer?

1. We are incurably religious. If we can't have the one true God, we will substitute gods. We must have Someone greater than we, one high above us, one to whom we can pray and worship. Humanity was not made to live apart from God.

2. False gods are our own making. They do not have an existence of their own. They are non-entities, utterly false. False gods are the product of our imaginations.

3. God knows what is going on in the world and in our lives. It was Yahweh who told Moses about the golden calf.

4. God's hiddenness does not mean abandonment. Because Moses was away for 40 days, the people thought he deserted them. The same can be thought of God. Though for a time we have a dry period and God is not as close as he once was does not mean God is dead.

5. Atonement can be made only by self-sacrifice. Moses understood this and thus he offered himself as a sacrifice for the sin of the people. Christ made atonement for us when he died on the cross. It was for us that he died.

6. Intercession in behalf of others is a vital part of prayer. We dare not pray for ourselves only. People are hurting and they need us to plead to God on their behalf.

7. Twice Moses confessed the "great sin." Confession of sins is a necessary part of prayer. Since we all sin, we all need to confess. We cannot approach God if we are covered with sin and guilt. Sin separates us from God. Prayer calls for an intimacy with God. As preparation for prayer, we should begin with confession and plead for forgiveness.

8. Because of Moses' intercessary prayer, Yahweh said he would forgive the people. To prove his forgiveness, Moses

was told to lead them to Canaan. However, there is judgment for sin committed. Every time a law is broken, there is a penalty. It happens in the state as well as in athletics. We can pull a nail out of furniture, but there remains a scar. Because God is justice as well as love, judgment follows sin.

David's Unanswered Prayer — 2 Samuel 7:18-29

It was the right time for David to build a temple. At least, he thought so. But, God had another plan. David was faced with what we often encounter: unanswered prayer. What do you do about that kind of prayer? Do you get angry with God or lose faith in him? Let us take a look at David's unanswered prayer and learn how we might handle the same.

Before reviewing David's prayer, we need to see it in its context. What made him offer this prayer? We need to go back to the beginning of chapter 7. The time was ripe to build a temple. David, a man of war, defeated all his enemies; he had no more kings to conquer. The land was at peace. When at war, it is no time to build a temple. You need all the manpower and materials you can get (7:1).

In addition, David tells his prophet-confidant, Nathan, that he feels bad about living in a house of cedar when the ark of God is in a tent (v. 2). He lives in a luxurious mansion and God lives in a tent, because the ark was identified with God. That is not right. His conscience hurts him. Is that any way to treat God? Therefore, David announces his plan to build a temple to house the ark. Nathan, the prophet of God, agrees with him (v. 3).

But, the plan did not please God. That very night the Lord gave a message to Nathan to take to David. David is not to build a temple. The Lord will do it. He promises he will do it through a son of David. He also promises that David's kingdom will last forever (v. 16).

So, David prays in response to the message from God spoken by Nathan. David sits down to pray (v. 18). Usually

33

people pray standing, kneeling, or prostrating. Perhaps David had much to pray about and needed to sit for the long haul. He wanted to talk over the problem of the temple with the Lord. You will notice that David sat "before the Lord" (v. 18). This is what true prayer is. It is being in the presence of God and having a conversation with him. True prayer is not talking to yourself.

David prays with humility. He asks God, "Who am I, O Lord God, and what is my house, that you have brought me thus far?" (v. 18). In this prayer David repeatedly refers to himself as a "servant" (v. 20). Can you imagine the humility? Here is David, Israel's greatest king and conquerer of his world, and yet before God he considers himself just a servant!

Moreover, his prayer is filled with praise and gratitude. The Lord has made David great. The Lord is even greater because "there is no one like you" (v. 22). David gives God all the credit for bringing the nation out of bondage to a prosperous land. He holds to God's promise that some day his son would build the temple. With a great spirit David asks God to bless his family and people.

What Can We Learn From David's Prayer?

1. The quality of the house of God should be equivalent to the houses of the people. People should not live in mansions while the church is in shambles. Only our very best is good enough for God.

2. Unanswered prayer may be a blessing. In refusing David's prayer, God gave a temple far better than what David might have built. When God says, "No," he may have something better for us.

3. A prophet may be wrong. After all a prophet is a human and humans are known to fail. Nathan agreed with David's plan but later God reversed it.

4. David took his defeat with all grace. He did not get angry with God or disown him as his God. Instead, he praised and thanked God for the good God had done for him and his

people. Our prayers need to be filled with praise, thanks, and adoration, for God is so good to us.

5. We cannot live happily nor satisfactorily unless God blesses us. Like David, we plead for God's continued blessing throughout life.

Solomon's Wise Choice — 1 Kings 3:3-14

How much wisdom can a child of 14 have? Enough to govern a great nation? According to Josephus, Solomon was only 14 when he offered this prayer for wisdom!

Solomon succeeded his father, David, as king of Israel. Solomon was seated on his father's throne, married to Pharaoh's sister, and completed building his mansion and the temple (3:1). Because as yet the worship of the land was not centralized in Jerusalem, Solomon offered sacrifices at high places such as Gibeon (3:2). Solomon loved the Lord and obeyed his father's commands. His love was demonstrated by his offering 1,000 burnt sacrifices (v. 4).

While worshipping at Gibeon the Lord came to Solomon one night in a dream and asked him the $64,000 question, "Ask what I should give you" (v. 5). Solomon did not answer at once from the top of his head. Instead he talked about God's love for David and what God had done for his father. Then he mentions the fact that God made him his father's successor. Solomon claimed he was only a child and did not know whether he was coming or going (v. 7). Then he gets around to saying what he wanted: "an understanding mind" and the ability to tell the difference between good and evil (v. 9).

Again, as in the case of Jacob, Moses, and David, the Lord comes to Solomon, this time in a dream. In the prayer that follows we see that Solomon included thanks and praise for God's goodness. In his dealing with God, he expressed his humility by saying he felt inadequate for this high calling to govern a mighty nation. His one request was for wisdom. And did God answer that prayer! There were two prostitutes who came to Solomon. Each claimed the living baby was hers. Solomon ordered a guard to cut the child in half and give one part to each mother. One woman agreed to it, but the other begged for the child's life. By this Solomon knew who was the true mother. For a further account of Solomon's wisdom, read 1 Kings 4:29-34.

What was God's response to Solomon's request? "It pleased the Lord" (v. 10). God was happy that Solomon did not ask for wealth, power, nor longevity. Thus, God gave him wisdom like none other in history except Jesus. In addition, the Lord added to wisdom the gifts of wealth and honor (v. 13). It reminds us of Jesus' teaching, "Strive first for the kingdom of heaven and his righteousness and all these things will be given to you as well" (Matthew 6:33). However, there is one condition for the continuation of these gifts: "If you will walk in my ways and keep my commandments ..." (v. 14).

What Can We Learn From Solomon's Prayer?

1. We pray because God first comes to us and talks with us as the Lord came to Solomon in a dream. Solomon was in the right atmosphere for God to speak to him — worship at Gibeon. For us, God speaks to us in and through his Word recorded in the Bible. Before we begin to pray, we need to listen to God and then respond.

2. Here we have a case of prayer as dialogue. First, God speaks to Solomon. He then responds. Finally God has the last word. Prayer can be a dialogue, because basically prayer is communication between God and the believer.

3. Solomon already had the wisdom to ask for the right and best thing God could give him. In our prayers we ask for many things. Are they all wise? needful? unselfish? Solomon did not ask wisdom for his own use or welfare but that he might be a good ruler.

4. The goal of everyone who prays should have the goal of pleasing God by what we ask. Think over your prayers. Are they all well-pleasing to God?

5. There is a catch to getting God's blessings in the future. As he told Solomon, blessings will come *if* we will keep the laws of God. If not, there is judgment to come. With judgment come defeat and death. This emphasizes the indispensability of obedience to God's will.

Reflection/Discussion

1. What makes a prayer pleasing to God?
2. What is your greatest request of God — wisdom?
3. Is unanswered prayer all bad?
4. How long is it sensible to persist in prayer?
5. Does one have a choice of gods?
6. Does God's hiddenness imply God's abandoment?

"Lord, make me an instrument of Thy peace, where there is hatred, let me sow love; where there is injury, pardon; where there is doubt, faith; where there is despair, hope; where there is darkness, light; and where there is sadness, joy. O divine Master, grant that I may not so much seek to be consoled as to console, to be understood, as to understand, to be loved as to love, for it is in giving that we receive; it is in pardoning that we are pardoned, and it is in dying that we are born to eternal life."

— St. Francis of Assisi

4
Requirements Of Effective Prayer

In this chapter we face several basic questions about prayer:
Why should I pray?
How do I get my prayers answered?
Am I praying aright to get the benefits of prayer?
What are the requirements of effective prayer?
These questions indicate that prayer does not come automatically nor by magic. There are conditions to be met. Prayer is a cooperative venture in which both the divine and human persons have parts to perform. God is faithful to do his part. Our part is meeting certain requirements to gain effective prayer.

The Requirement Of Faith

If there is no faith in God's existence, why pray? Would one want to talk to a non-existent being? If there is no faith in God or prayer, there is no use of praying. A person of faith is a person of prayer, and a person of prayer is a person of faith. They are inseparable. Faith is a requirement given by Jesus: "What ever you ask for in prayer with *faith* you will receive" (Matthew 21:22). Luther accepted this requirement: "Prayer is the work of faith alone which none but the Christian can do." At a critical time during the Civil War, President Lincoln had faith that God would save the Union. He explained: "I went to my room and got down in prayer. Never before had I prayed with such earnestness. I knew that defeat in a great battle on Northern soil involved loss of Washington and intervention of England and France in favor of the

Southern Confederacy. I felt that I must put all my trust in Almighty God. He gave our people the best country ever given to men. He alone could save it from destruction.''

It is a faith in a God who *hears* prayer. It is a faith in a personal, living, concerned God. It takes a heap of faith to believe that an almighty, transcendent, invisible, and incomprehensible God would listen to one of five billion people on earth. The miracle is that each of us, though least of the least, can approach this infinite God and by faith can have access to him. Because God is our Father and we are his children by adoption, we can come to God with confidence and cheerfulness. This is a father-child relationship in which the child is welcomed and heard. If there is no relationship, prayer is impossible. William James once admitted: ''I have no living sense of communion with God.'' Since prayer is communion with God, he apparently had no prayer life. This relationship is based on faith. It must not be a second-hand faith. A physician in one of my former churches was considered an active member who with his family attended worship services and served on the governing board of the congregation. After his death, his widow told me that a few months before his death, he had an experience with Jesus. Because of it, he came alive in faith and was prepared to die. His second-hand faith became a first-hand experience.

It is not only a faith that God hears prayer but also *answers* prayer. It is faith in a God who is aware of our needs and cares about our predicament. It was this kind of God who called Moses to return to Egypt to lead God's people out of slavery. God said to Moses, ''I have observed the misery of my people ... I have heard their cry ... I know of their sufferings, and I have come down to deliver them'' (Exodus 3:7, 8).

There are times when we do not believe God will answer our prayers. At a time of severe drought, a congregation gathered for a special meeting to pray for rain. When the preacher saw that they came without umbrellas, he upbraided them for their lack of faith. A similar lack of faith occurred at the time Peter was imprisoned. The Christians gathered to pray for Peter's release. He was given his freedom and Peter came to the house where they were praying for him. He knocked on the door and Rhoda recognized Peter's voice. She ran back to tell the assembly that Peter was free. They said she was crazy. When Peter continued knocking, they finally opened the door and let Peter in. They did not believe that their prayer would be answered.

A necessary ingredient for effective prayer is the kind of faith a little girl had. She was lost in a farmer's meadow. He found her and comforted her by saying, "Don't cry. I will take you home." With a smile she snuggled up to him and said, "I knew you would come; I was waiting for you." "Waiting for me? What made you think I was coming?" She replied, "I was praying that you would."

In Jesus' Name

Jesus gives a second condition for effective prayer. In his last discourse with his Disciples before his passion he told them, "If you ask anything of the Father in my name, he will give it to you" (John 16:23).

It seems that to get a prayer answered all you have to say is three little words, "In Jesus' name." It is really not as simple or magical as that. What's in a name? In Biblical usage, a name is identified with the person. A name not only identifies the person but describes the nature of the person. To say "In Jesus' name" is the same as calling upon Jesus to answer the prayer.

The name of Jesus means that he is our intercessor. He is seated at the right hand of the Father and intercedes for us. He takes our requests to God. Therefore, we do not pray directly to God but to Christ who is our intermediary. Accordingly, our prayers may end "through Jesus Christ our Lord." He speaks for us and pleads to the Father in our behalf. He is our advocate, friend and helper. Therefore, God answers our prayers not for our sakes but for Jesus' sake. We have no merits that would move God to hear and answer our prayers, but we plead for an answer based on the merits of Jesus. In our secular life we use an intermediary when we feel we cannot get an audience with the person whom we think is too high and mighty. We get a friend to speak for us, to ask in our behalf. If a child wants to spend a night with a friend, she knows her mother will refuse. But, if her friend will ask for her, chances are good that her mother will not be able to say "no" to the friend.

To pray in Jesus' name means that this prayer is in accordance with what Jesus would pray. In addition, this prayer is offered in the spirit of Jesus. This kind of prayer would be unselfish and considerate of the welfare of all concerned. The spirit of this prayer would be the spirit of faith in and love for God. We, therefore, cannot pray for anything Jesus would not pray for. The prayer must have Jesus' approval before he can present it to the Father. To pray in Jesus' name is to pray a distinctive Christian prayer. Only Christians end their prayers in Jesus' name or through Jesus. No other religion prays with these words simply because no other religion has faith in Jesus as the Christ, the Son of God.

According To God's Will

A more difficult requirement for effective prayer is to pray according to God's will. In 1 John 5:14 we are given the requirement: "If we ask anything according to his will, he hears us."

God will not and cannot answer a prayer that goes against his will. In Gethsemane Jesus had the problem of finding God's will and conforming to it. His victory came when he prayed, "Not my will but thine be done." We should not pray to get God to do our will but to get our wills to harmonize with his will. We do not pray, "Thy will be changed" but "Thy will be done." To harmonize our wills with God's will may be most difficult especially if we are strong-willed people. It was not easy for Jesus, for he was in great distress and his sweat was like drops of blood falling to the ground. It is like tuning up violin strings which must be stretched almost to the breaking point in order for the strings to be in tune. In prayer our souls may likewise be put under such pressure and tension until our wills coincide with God's will.

The problem for many of us is not only to pray according to God's will but to know what the will of God is for our lives in a particular situation. We are never sure and so we pray, "If it is your will." What is God's will for my life's work, or my life partner? Should I marry? Change jobs? Have a baby? Get a divorce? Whatever it is, God's will is always good. The will of One who died for us on a cross is always for our welfare. Therefore, we should never dread to do God's will but rather rejoice that what he wants us to do is for our best interests.

Persistent Prayer

Jesus gives us another condition for effective prayer. The requirement is persistence: pray and again pray and pray again. Keep at it. Don't become weary in praying. Luke records, "Then Jesus told them a parable about their need to pray always and not to lose heart" (Luke 18:1). In addition, Jesus taught two parables on persistent prayer. One was about a friend who came at midnight and asked for bread to feed his unexpected guests. At first the man declined to get up and give him bread, but the friend kept begging so that the man gave in to his plea (Luke 11:5-8). The other parable was about a widow who persistently came to a judge to get justice. At first he would not listen to her, but over and over she called for justice. In order to keep her from wearing him out, he granted her appeal. In both cases persistence won out.

There are other classic cases of persistence in prayer. Jacob struggled all night with an angel. Jacob said, "I will not let you go until you bless me." Jesus practiced what he taught about persistence. In the Garden he did not pray once to have the cup of death pass away from him but three times. Monica, the mother of St. Augustine, prayed for her son to become a Christian over a period of 30 years. Her reprobate son became one of the church's most famous theologians. Persistent prayer accomplishes great things.

Why do we have to persist in our prayers? Why doesn't God answer the first time we beg for a blessing? Is God reluctant to answer and must he be persuaded to help us? Consider the following answers. First, we need to persist because we may not be ready for God's answer. It is like a boy asking for a 22 gun when he was too young to handle a gun responsibly. Second, God may not be able to answer the prayer for lack of human cooperation. God often answers a prayer through people. A wife may pray that her husband lose his taste for liquor and thereby cease to be an alcoholic. For the prayer to be answered, the husband must cooperate with God by probably joining AA. Or, a mother may pray for her teenage daughter to be free from drugs. But, God cannot answer the prayer because the girl refuses to listen to God. Third, if we do not persist in praying, we may not be receptive when the time comes for God to answer the prayer. If we keep on praying, we will be open and receptive for the answer that may come years later. Fourth, God may not answer our prayers immediately in order to test our faith in him. This was the case of the prayer of the Syrophoenician mother who persisted in crying to Jesus to heal her daughter. Though the Disciples asked Jesus to send her away, though Jesus said he was sent to Jews only, though Jesus said it was not fair to give children's food to dogs, Jesus finally gave in and said, "Women, great is your faith."

Praying With Humility

A western rancher asked the District Superintendent of his church to assign a pastor to his community. "How big a man do you want?" asked the Superintendent. "Well," the rancher replied, "we're not overly particular, but when he's on his knees we'd like him to reach heaven." Humility is expressed in kneeling. Since few churches provide kneelers for prayers, we are a pretty proud people. As Jesus taught, the humble will be exalted. When we are on our knees, we are tall enough to reach heaven.

Jesus taught a lesson on humility for prayer. He told of two men who went to the temple to pray. The one, a Pharisee, was a proud man. In his prayer five times he told God the good he had done. The other one, a Publican, was so humble he would not even look up to heaven. He beat his chest and begged, "God, be merciful to me a sinner" (Luke 18:9-14). What was the result? The humble man went home with an answered prayer.

These days it is popular to be proud. Have you ever noticed bumper stickers telling the world how proud we are of our children's school honors and of our athletic teams? One day Harry Emerson Fosdick met a couple of parishioners while taking a walk near his Riverdale church in New York City. He greeted the mother and her four-year-old daughter. When they parted, Fosdick said to the little girl, "Tell your daddy that you spoke to Dr. Harry Emerson Fosdick this morning." To which the child responded, "And you tell your mommy that you talked to Susie Smith."

On the other hand, there are humble people. An aide of President Clinton expressed his humility when he said, "I am the monkey; he is the organ grinder." One of the greatest prayers was composed by St. Francis of Assisi. He began his prayer, "Lord, make me an instrument of Thy peace." In humility he thought of himself only as an "instrument." Have you ever gone to a piano recital? The pianist was excellent. The music was wonderful. The audience thundered their approval. But, what about the piano, the instrument? Nobody clapped for the piano. It was only an instrument that displayed the talent of the pianist and revealed the wonder of the music. Humility is the piano as an instrument. It gets no praise. It is content to be used.

Effective prayer calls for humility. It is expressed when we confess our sins and cry, "Lord, have mercy." When we praise God, we express our humility, for we are praising God and not ourselves. When we thank God, we are humble to acknowledge that all that we are and have came from God. In prayer we express our humility by telling God that we deserve nothing, that we are not worthy to receive his blessings. In humility we throw ourselves on God's mercy. And remember, the humble Publican went home justified rather than the proud Pharisee.

The Spirit In Prayer

It is impossible to pray adequately without the Holy Spirit. We do not know how to pray or what to pray for. The Spirit of God comes to our rescue. Paul in Romans 8:26-27 admits that he does not know how to pray as he ought. He knows how to preach, how to teach, how to write letters to his congregations. He knows how to love and serve. The one thing he does not know is how to pray. In this passage he assures us that the Spirit helps us to pray aright.

How does the Holy Spirit help us in our praying? Paul says the Spirit intercedes for us when we do not know what or how to pray. The Spirit prays in our behalf and pleads our case before the throne of God. Moreover, the Spirit reveals to us the mind of God and knows the will of God. Therefore, when the Spirit prays in and for us, we pray as we should. Before we pray, we need to invoke God's Spirit to come to us and pray for us.

Our Part In Answering Prayers

It is not enough to pray to God to solve a problem or answer a need. We need to do something about what we prayed. We are partners with God. Some things God cannot do by

46

himself. He needs human cooperation. Often he answers prayer through and with people. Bound with two chains and sleeping between two guards, Peter was imprisoned by King Herod for preaching the Gospel. In the middle of the night when all were sleeping, an angel opened the prison door and awakened Peter. The angel removed the chains from Peter, and told Peter to help himself: "Fasten your belt and put on your sandals. Wrap your cloak around you and follow me" (Acts 12:6-11). God wants us to do what we can to answer our own prayers.

It is not enough to pray that the hungry be fed. God expects us to bring food to the malnourished. We may pray for the one in every seven Americans living below the poverty line, and the 50 percent of American illiterate adults, and the 37 million people without health insurance. All well and good! But, how will God answer our prayers in their behalf unless we do our part to relieve those needs and change the conditions that cause the poverty, hunger, and illness?

The answer is in the story of a little girl's brother who set a trap to catch birds. She felt it was wrong and cruel to trap birds. At first she cried about it but later became happy. Her mother asked her why she was so happy. She explained, "I prayed for my brother to be a better boy." "And what else?" "I prayed that his trap would not catch birds." "And what else?" "Well, then I went out and kicked the trap to pieces."

Unanswered Prayers

If the seven foregoing conditions for effective prayer are met, why are some prayers not answered? In one sense every prayer is answered: Yes, No, Wait, and Be surprised! There are times when God says "no" to our requests. It may be a comfort to you to know that Jesus experienced unanswered prayers. One time he said to Peter, "I have prayed for you that your faith may not fail" (Luke 22:32). But, Peter's faith did fail when three times he denied he knew Jesus. In Gethsemane Jesus prayed three times that he would be saved from

47

going to the cross. But, it was God's will for him to die as a sacrifice for our sin. Jesus submitted to the Father's will: "Not my will but Thine be done." St. Paul had a similar experience. Three times he prayed that the thorn in his flesh would be removed. Each time God answered, "My grace is sufficient for you" (2 Corinthians 12:7-9).

Thanks be to God for unanswered prayer! P. T. Forsyth wrote: "We shall come one day to a heaven where we shall gratefully know that God's great refusals were sometimes the true answers to our truest prayer." We can be grateful, for we may pray for what we want rather than what we need. What we want may not be good for us. Again, what we pray for may not be in accord with God's will and therefore God cannot violate his own will. What we pray for may not be for our good. Ruth, the wife of Billy Graham, thanked God for not answering her prayer when she was courted by suitors before she fell in love with Billy. What a mistake, she felt, if she had married another man!

What are some of the reasons for unanswered prayer? The Bible says sin causes it. "If I had cherished iniquity in my heart, the Lord would not have listened" (Psalm 66:18). "It is because of your sin that he doesn't hear you" (Isaiah 59:2). "The prayer of the righteous is powerful and effective" (James 5:16). When the great Raphael worked on a painting, he wore a candle in a pasteboard cap so that his shadow would not fall on his work. Some prayers are spoiled because the pray-er's own shadow of sin falls on the prayer. A person who prays needs to wear a candle of renunciation of sin.

Another reason for unanswered prayer is the offering of wrong requests. James wrote, "You ask and do not receive, because you ask wrongly in order to spend what you get on your pleasures" (James 4:3). A wrong request may be one for revenge. Listen to Jeremiah's prayer for revenge on his enemies: famine, childlessness, pestilence, and death (Jeremiah 18:19-23). When I was serving a church some years ago, one of my members asked me to marry him and his Roman Catholic fiance. Her mother was furious that I consented to marry

48

the couple. She did not want a mixed marriage in her family. After the wedding she wrote me, "I shall pray every day that one of your daughters will break your heart as mine is broken." I thank God her prayer was not answered.

A wrong request may be a selfish prayer filled with "I," "me," and "mine." A child's prayer was a selfish one:

> *"Now I lay me down to sleep.*
> *I pray the Lord my soul to keep,*
> *And if I die before I wake,*
> *I pray the Lord my toys to break,*
> *So none of the kids can use 'em."*

God may surprise us with a different answer which is even better than what we wanted. An anonymous author prayed:

> *"He asked for strength that he might achieve;*
> *He was made weak that he might obey.*
> *He asked for health that he might do greater things;*
> *He was given infirmity that he might do better things.*
> *He asked for riches that he might be happy;*
> *He was given poverty that he might be wise.*
> *He asked for power that he might have the praise of men;*
> *He was given weakness that he might feel the need of God.*
> *He asked for all things that he might enjoy life;*
> *He was given life that he might enjoy all things."*

Reflection/Discussion

1. Are there exceptions to Jesus' promise, "If you ask anything"?

2. Does God answer non-Christian prayers?

3. What makes you think that an infinite God would listen to a microscopic biped on planet earth, a tiny planet among millions upon millions of greater stars?

4. Is it appropriate to conclude a prayer in Jesus' name when the prayer is offered in a religiously mixed audience?

5. Have you ever thanked God for not answering your prayer?

6. If faith is required to pray effectively, where does one get faith?

"Almighty God, unto whom all hearts are open, all desires known, and from whom no secrets are hid: cleanse the thoughts of our hearts by the inspiration of Thy Holy Spirit that we may perfectly love Thee and worthily magnify Thy holy name through Christ our Lord. Amen."

— Book of Common Prayer

5
The Content
Of Prayer

What do you say to God in prayer? What should you pray for? Our answers deal with the content of our prayers. In this chapter these questions are for our consideration.

1. Is it selfish to pray for self? If it is selfish, then we should offer selfless prayers. Is a selfless prayer a complete prayer?

2. When praying for others, does the person want or need what we are asking?

3. Is prayer more than just asking for favors?

4. Do we pray for the right things that harmonize with God's will? At the last minute a pastor realized he forgot to invite a little old lady to his garden party. He phoned her and pleaded for her to come. "It's no use," she told him. "I have already prayed for rain."

5. Do we pray for insignificant incidentals? A woman prays for a parking space at a mall. Because he cannot make up his mind, a man prays for God to tell him which of two ties to buy. A youth goes to an ice cream shoppe and prays for guidance whether to order chocolate or vanilla. Would you call that a trivial pursuit in prayer?

6. When called upon to lead a group in prayer, are you at a loss to know what to pray for? Does not knowing what to pray cause you to decline the invitation?

Structures For Prayer's Contents

To keep our prayers from rambling, repeating, and being a hodge-podge, we need a structure or outline to follow.

One structure easy to remember is the word ACTSS. It serves as an acrostic with each letter representing a subject for prayer. "A" stands for adoration or awe. This results from our conception of the greatness of God. We stand in awe of him. There is a mystery about him. Adoration is the spontaneous yearning of the heart to worship, honor, magnify, and bless God. This leads to thanksgiving and praise for his endless blessings. When we adore God, we magnify the Lord. Words fail us to express our wonder at his greatness, goodness and grace. Adoration is the joyous celebration of God. The Virgin Mary sang, "My soul proclaims the greatness of the Lord; my spirit rejoices in God my Savior." Zechariah, filled with adoration, also sang, "Blessed be the Lord God of Israel."

"C" stands for confession. Confession can be of two kinds: faith and sin. In prayer we can tell God that we believe in him, in his good will, and in his plan for our lives. Confession of sin is necessary, for sin blocks the entrance into God's presence. Upon our confession of sin, God is faithful and just to forgive us.

"T" is for thanksgiving. When we count our blessings, we voluntarily and instinctively pour out our thanks. The more we recognize God's gifts, the less we have to ask him for benefits. Why did Jesus command us to pray? Luther answered: "The reason he commands it is, of course, not in order to have us acknowledge and confess that he is already bestowing many blessings on us and that he can and will give us still more."

"S" calls for us to pray in terms of supplication. It is our response to Jesus' teaching: "Ask and it will be given you" (Luke 11:9). Supplication refers to the petitions for self and others. Prayer is asking God for his blessings. If we do not ask, the blessings will not be received. Henry Ford once bought an insurance policy so large it attracted public attention. A friend, an insurance salesman, asked him, "Didn't you know I sell insurance?" "Yes, of course," replied Ford. "Then why didn't you buy it from me?" Ford explained, "You never asked me."

The extra "S" stands for submission. Our wills do not always correspond to God's will. Therefore, with Jesus we say, "Not my will but Thine be done." When we realize that God's will is always good for us, that God is for us and is on our side, we will be content to submit gladly to do his will.

A House Of Prayer

Leslie Weatherhead in his book, *A Private House Of Prayer*, suggests that the structure of the content of prayer be likened to a house of seven rooms. Each room is a division of prayer. There may be some duplication with ACTSS which we just discussed.

The first room is for the affirmation of God's presence. If prayer is a conversation with God, obviously it is necessary for him to be present. When we pray, are we aware of his presence or like Moses do we see only a burning bush? In a hymn Tersteegen sings, "God himself is present; let us now adore him and with awe appear before him." What applies to worship, applies also to prayer. When we pray, we are talking to a real person, not to an idea, or ideal, or ideology, or a theological concept. In prayer we are not talking to ourselves or to the ceiling. In spirit God is there to hear our prayer. We need to realize this and pray accordingly.

The next room is for the thanksgiving and praise. We have been blessed beyond measure and therefore to thank and praise God is in order. Before we begin our prayer, we need to review how good God has been to us. If we are bereft of blessings, our greatest gift is Jesus who loved us enough to die for us.

Go to the next room for the confession of sins. Sin separates us from God. Sin erects an impenetrable curtain which prevents us from seeing God. The separation prevents our hearing the voice of God. We come out of a dirty world with the dirt of sin clinging to us. Before we can be presentable to a holy God we need spiritual cleansing. Thus, in prayer we confess our sins and plead for his mercy.

53

The fourth room is labelled "Reception of God's grace." We have confessed our sins and begged for mercy. What is God's response? It is grace in terms of pardon and acceptance. At this time in our prayers we remember his promises to be with us always, to forgive us, and to bless us with the Holy Spirit.

Now it is time to go to the room of petition. We have the opportunity to tell God about our personal needs in our own lives, or in our family, or in our work. But, we have petitions not only for ourselves, but others want and need our prayers in their behalf. This takes us to the sixth room of prayer. When we pray for others, it is called intercessory prayer. When his co-worker, Melanchthon, was sick, Luther prayed for him: "I besought the Almighty with great vigor ... quoting from Scripture all the promises I could remember, that prayers should be granted and said that he must grant my prayer, if I was henceforth to put faith in his promises."

The effectiveness of a friend's prayer on our behalf depends on the relationship of the pray-er to God. James wrote, "The prayer of the righteous is powerful and effective" (James 5:16). That is why we want a godly mother or a pious pastor to pray for us. Roman Catholics ask the saints and the Virgin Mary to pray for them. On the eve of a historic boxing match, a friend was visiting the champ in his hotel suite. During the conversation a murmuring feminine voice was heard. "That's my wife," the champ explained. "She's praying for me to win." "Oh, and I suppose you pray, too?" The champ replied, "My wife is more devout than I am. If God won't do it for her, He certainly won't do it for me."

The seventh room in the house of prayer is meditation. Some do not understand what meditation is and consequently do not know how to meditate. It is the act of reflecting, of silence, and listening to God. It calls for thinking about God and our relationship to him. It is a time to review past dealings with God. Then we reflect on how good God has been in those past dealings. After that, we remember God's promises to us: promises of peace, protection, and provision. Meditation can be summed up in three R's: review, reflect, and remember.

A Staircase Of Prayer

When we are about to compose a prayer, another structure for the content can be likened to a staircase from earth to heaven. Jacob had this experience when in his prayer he saw angels descending and ascending on a ladder extending from his head to heaven. Arthur John Gossip suggests a staircase of seven steps comparable to Weatherhead's seven-room house of prayer.

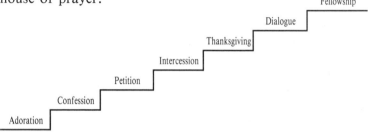

This diagram illustrates the different levels of prayer. There are some aspects of prayer more worthy and effective than the lower levels. The highest form of prayer is fellowship with God. That means prayer is more important than petition or intercession. A child once sent a letter to God asking: "Dear God, Is it okay to talk to you even when I don't want anything? Love, Eric." Fellowship with God is an ongoing and growing relationship with God that transcends time or petition. Prayer is about being, not primarily about doing. It is being alone in God's presence just as Jesus frequently went to a lonely place to commune with his Father. Prayer can be a non-verbal communion of just being in each other's presence. In this sense, we can pray without ceasing by practicing the presence of God every hour.

Next to fellowship is dialogue. This is based on the level of conversation. Prayer is not talking to God but *with* God. It is a two-way conversation. For some prayer is a monologue with the person doing all the talking to God. It is like answering your telephone: you do all the talking and then hang up. God is not given a chance to talk with you. If it is going to be a fellowship, a dialogue, we must listen and be quiet. How does God speak to us? To be sure it is God and not Satan speaking to us, we go to the Word, the holy Scriptures. Therefore, Bible reading should precede praying.

The Hand Of Prayer

Perhaps the easiest way to organize our prayers is to pattern the prayer after the human hand. Stretch out your hand and your fingers will remind you what or whom to pray for.

Thumb — It is closest to you. Pray for those near and dear to you.

Index finger — Pray for your teachers/leaders who customarily use that finger when pointing out facts and figures.

Middle finger — It is your largest finger. Pray for the important people in your life and society: rulers, governors, legislators, judges, president.

Weakest finger — This is the weakest one on your hand. It reminds us to pray for weak people: the handicapped, sick, and needy.

Little finger — Your smallest finger represents you. In humility pray for yourself.

This raises the question whether we should pray for ourselves. It is apparently okay to pray for yourself, because Jesus did. In John 17:1 he prayed, "Father, the hour has come; glorify your Son that the Son may glorify you." You will notice that it was not a selfish prayer. He asked his Father to glorify him only because he wanted to glorify his Father. When praying for ourselves, there is a temptation to pray selfishly. Phillips Brooks tells us how to pray for ourselves: "Oh, do not pray for easy lives. Pray to be stronger men (and women)! Do not pray for tasks equal to your powers. Pray for powers equal to your tasks. Then the doing of your work shall be no miracle. Every day you shall wonder at yourself, at the richness of life which has come to you by the grace of God."

Praying For Others

The content of prayer contains both prayers for self and others. Some ask us to pray for them. They say, "Please pray for me." Even godly people, who are experts in praying, want our prayers. Jesus took his three Disciples with him into the Garden of Gethsemane to pray for him. When he found them sleeping instead of praying, he said, "Stay awake and pray" (Matthew 26:41). St. Paul felt the need of prayer and urged his fellow-believers to pray for him as he did in his letter to the Ephesians: "Pray also for me, so that when I speak, a message may be given to me to make known with boldness the mystery of the gospel" (Ephesians 6:19). Martin Luther invariably ended his letters with "Remember to pray for me," or "Vale, ora pro me," "Farewell, pray for me."

People not only ask for our prayers but need our prayers. The sick need us to pray for them. James asks, "Are any among you sick? They should call for the elders of the church and have them pray over them ..." (James 5:14). When one is seriously ill, it is very difficult to collect one's thoughts and to concentrate enough to pray. The sick may be sedated and cannot think clearly. In a weakened condition the sick cannot formulate thoughts or find words for the thoughts. I did not realize this until I was in the hospital for brain surgery following an auto accident. Never before did I realize the importance of having a pastor come and pray for you. It is the same when your dearest dies. You are shocked with grief. You cannot think for crying. Bereavement can be a traumatic experience. At a time like this, we need a pastor or friend to do our praying. Pastors, too, want and need the prayers of their congregations. They cannot do the work alone: to speak for God, to live a Christlike life, to perform the many tasks of preaching, teaching, counselling, and pastoring. Also, the nation needs our prayers at a time when crime is on a rampage, AIDS is in an epidemic stage, when millions are unemployed, when drug addiction is a common condition, and children are illegitimately bearing children.

On the other hand, some may not want to be prayed for. Therefore, it is wise to ask a person if he/she would like you to pray. It is reported that when Tallulah Bankhead was close to death, her housekeeper sat by her bed and whispered prayers. When Tallulah heard the praying, she exploded, "Damn it! Don't you dare pray for me." Sometimes people do not want you to pray for certain things for them. A pastor said to a woman, "Now just say to God: Let anything happen to me that you want to happen to me." She replied, "Oh no! I don't want that!"

How then are we to pray for others? There is a temptation to pray in generalities such as "for all sorts and conditions of men." We can mention the sick and the sorrowing, the oppressed and the poor. While we cover almost everybody with these words, we do not contact anybody individually. In Exodus there is a description of Aaron's breastplate worn when he entered the holy of holies. On it was engraved the names of the 12 tribes of Israel (Exodus 28:21, 29). Pray specifically by name: for Karen in the hospital, for Nancy with arthritis, for Mary with a malignancy, for Harold with lung cancer, and for Bill with a stroke.

Some churches have prayer wheels. A group of people dedicate themselves to pray daily for members in need of prayer. When a person gets sick or has a problem, his/her name is put on the wheel. And round and round goes the wheel from one pray-er to the next.

Individuals often keep a personal prayer list. At the time of prayer one cannot always remember the many people needing prayer. The list is kept at the place of prayer and one by one is prayed for by name.

When we pray for others, we need to pray in faith for them. Believe God hears and answers the prayers offered for others. Remember what Job's prayer did for his friends: "My servant Job shall pray for you, for I will accept his prayer not to deal with you according to your folly."

And we need to keep praying for others lest we sin by not doing so. Praying for others is a sacred obligation. Samuel told his people, "Far be it from me that I should sin against the Lord by ceasing to pray for you" (1 Samuel 12:23).

How can we get God to answer our prayers? Shall we threaten him as a Roman Catholic boy once did? He wanted a bicycle very badly. His mother told them they were too poor to buy him a bicycle. Rather she told him to pray for one. That night he lighted a candle before a statue of the Virgin Mary and wrote her a note: "Dear Virgin Mary, I need a bicycle very badly." The next night he did the same and wrote, "Dear Virgin Mary, I must have a bicycle." The next night he took the statue down, rolled it in a bedspread, and stuffed it in a drawer. This time he wrote to Jesus: "Dear Jesus, if you ever want to see your mother again —"

Or shall we bargain with God as Abraham did regarding the righteous in the sin city of Sodom? Or, maybe we can make a deal with God. If he will bless us, as Jacob said, then we will tithe and worship him (Genesis 28:20-22). Or, maybe we can make a bold promise to God to reform, to stop sinning, or to give a big gift to the church if he will get us out of trouble. Only when the blessing comes, we quickly forget to fulfill the promise.

According to Scripture, we cannot force or bargain with God to get his favor and the answer to our prayers. God is more willing to give than we are to pray. If we ask in humility and faith, in accordance with his will, and in the name of Jesus, we can be sure our prayers will be answered.

Reflection/Discussion

1. If God is all-knowing and all-compassionate, why pray for help?

2. If a person has no need, what good is prayer?

3. How does one's conception of God affect prayer?

4. Is it necessary to bargain with God to gain a favor?

5. Is it a sin not to pray for others?

6. Are there times when one's physical or mental condition makes one unable to pray?

"O God, who makest the minds of the faithful to be of one will: Grant unto Thy people that they may love what Thou commandest, and desire what Thou dost promise; that, among the manifold changes of this world, our hearts may there be fixed where true joys are to be found; through Jesus Christ our Lord, who liveth and reigneth with Thee and the Holy Spirit, one God, world without end. Amen."

— An ancient Collect

6
The Mechanics
Of Prayer

Our goal is to pray like Jesus. We want to improve the effectiveness of our prayers. That is our objective, but what are the means of reaching the goal? We have come to the time when we need to consider the nuts and bolts of Christlike prayer. What do we say? When do we say it? Where do we say it? How long should we pray? How often? These are some of the mechanics of prayer. They are important as means to the end.

The Time Element

What should the duration of prayer be? How much time should be devoted to prayer? How much time do you have for prayer? It depends on the kind of prayer. A sentence prayer takes less than a minute. An arrow prayer takes even less time. But, when prayer involves Bible reading, reflection, and meditation, you are talking about a block of time.

Great Christians of the past spent hours in prayer. Martin Luther gave three hours per day for prayer. He explained, "I have so much business I cannot get on without spending three hours daily in prayer." John Wesley spent two hours daily in prayer and would let nothing take that time away from him. On the front page of each of his daily journals, he recorded his resolution to spend two hours daily in private prayer.

It seems unrealistic for the average busy person in today's world to take hours for prayer. Who among us could afford that much time and properly take care of homes, business, and personal responsibilities? If you had two or three hours daily for prayer, would you know how to profitably use that time?

Our brief prayers may explain why today we do not have spiritual giants. They derived their power and motivation from God in prayer. If we are too busy to spend time with God, we are too busy and our souls suffer for it. If the average American watches TV seven hours a day, is it too much to expect a Christian to spend one hour a day in prayer?

Times Of Prayer

The prophet Daniel prayed three times a day. Is that too often for a modern person? Some have difficulty finding time to pray once a day. When are the times we might pray?

Morning is a good time to pray. The Psalmist thought so, too: "O Lord, in the morning you hear my voice; in the morning I plead my case to you and watch" (Psalm 5:3). In an interview Mother Teresa was asked, "What did you do this morning?" Answer: "Pray." "When did you start?" "Half past four." Morning is an excellent time for prayer because it gives you strength for what follows throughout the day. A jeweler asked a friend who had a fine Swiss watch, "When do you wind your watch?" "Why, at night, before I retire," replied the friend. "Oh," said the jeweler, "a watch should be wound in the morning, so that it can start the day on a strong spring. It would then be prepared against the bumps and shocks of the day." What is good for a watch is good for the soul. In the morning by prayer you can get in tune with God and ask for strength and wisdom to handle whatever the day may bring. After the morning prayer, you can confidently say, "Let's go for it!"

Bedtime is also a fitting time to pray. The bed makes a convenient "altar" before which you can kneel. At this time you can confess any mistakes you made that day, seek forgiveness, and be at peace with God. It is time to ask God to let his angels protect you from all harm and danger through the night. In trust you surrender yourself to God and put yourself in his care just as you put your whole trust in the bed to hold you up. Soon then you will fall asleep and rest the whole night through.

Prayer at meal times is an appropriate time to pray. It does not matter where you eat — in the privacy of your home or in a public restaurant, whether it is a silent or oral prayer. This is the time to acknowledge God as the giver of everything you are and have. Without this providence, you would starve.

A very important time for prayer is at personal or family devotions. The latter is almost a thing of the past even in Christian homes. Family devotions is the time when the family gathers together with God. Both parents and children take part in the devotions: Bible reading, a meditation, and prayer. Like nothing else, family devotions solidifies the family in God. The effect can be seen in the spirit of the home and in the quality of life. In addition, there is need for a time for personal devotions. It is the time when a person is alone with God for Bible reading, meditation, and prayer. Because we are neglecting our devotions, it is estimated that in America there is only a five percent spirituality.

Some people pray only when there is an urgent need. They wait until there is a life-threatening event such as an announcement that a family member or friend has a terminal illness. It seems this is what might be called a "foxhole" prayer. A pastor was talking to children in a Children's Home and asked if they ever prayed. "Oh yes." "Fine, do you pray when you get up in the morning?" "No." "Well, do you pray when you go to bed at night?" "No." "Do you pray before meals then?" "No." "But when do you pray?" The children responded, "When grown-ups get angry." It is fine to pray when there is a need, but prayer is more than an emergency alarm!

St. Paul would say that we should always pray: "Pray without ceasing" (1 Thessalonians 5:17). Is that realistic? How could one pray without stopping? Consider the constant prayer of a church secretary who had a life-changing influence upon John Killinger, professor of religion at Stamford University, when he was a teenager: "She prayed in the morning. She prayed at noon; she prayed in the evening. She prayed as she typed; she prayed as she filed; she prayed as she talked on the telephone. It was almost inconceivable to me that there was a time in the day, or possibly in the night, when she wasn't praying. I don't think I ever saw her without believing that she had been in prayer at most 10 seconds ago." You, too, can pray without ceasing if you live, work, and play always in the consciousness of God's presence. Prayer does not require words. It can be an attitude or spirit. Your work can be a prayer. Your recreation also can be a prayer if it is done in the spirit of Christ.

If we are to pray unceasingly, is it possible to pray too much? If the prayer is repeated endlessly, it becomes vain repetition which Jesus condemned. Luther tells of the situation in his monastery: "Our lay brothers in Erfurt had to pray 400 Our Fathers in one day for the canonical hours. Once a certain brother said, 'If I were our Lord God, I wouldn't like to hear what I alone must pray, to say nothing of having my ears filled with the babbling of all the brothers.' " That kind of praying is too much praying!

Whenever we pray, we need persistent regularity. We dare not pray only when we feel like it, or when the spirit moves us, or when a crisis occurs. Effective prayer calls for praying every day at the same time and in the same place. Each of us should have a daily date with God, a holy tryst.

The Place Of Prayer

In our homes we have certain places where we do certain things. We have a place to eat — a dining room. We have a place for fellowship — a living room. We have a place to relax — a den or family room. We have a place to sleep — a bedroom. We have a place to work — a home office. We have a place to play — a recreation or play room. But, where is the place to pray — a prayer room?

Where we pray is important. It adds or detracts from our prayer life. It needs to be a place that is quiet and free from

64

disturbances and interruptions. It is a place to be alone with God. Repeatedly Jesus left the Disciples and the crowd to be alone to pray. When he heard the execution of John the Baptist, he took a boat and went to a place to be by himself (Matthew 14:13). After feeding 5,000, Jesus sent his Disciples off in a boat while he dismissed the crowd and "went up the mountain by himself to pray" (Matthew 14:23). While the Israelites were in the wilderness for 40 years, Moses erected a tent far from the people and daily went to this little tent to meet with Yahweh. John Wesley had a little prayer room just off his bedroom where he began each day with prayer.

This place of prayer can help us in our prayers. It is where we go day after day and it becomes so familiar to us that the place with its furnishings no longer distracts us. We may have a religious picture, hanging, or quotation that provides atmosphere for prayer. When we were first married, Barbara and I had our personal devotions in a joint study, for Barbara also is a minister. Soon we found that it was not a good arrangement because the slightest movement — a chair, a cough, a sneeze, or even the turning of a page distracted us. Now we each go to a favorite place where each can be alone for Bible reading and prayer.

There is a variety of places where we can pray. There is no place that is perfect. Each of us needs to choose a place best for us. In the Bible we find a variety of places where people prayed.

Church or temple. When King Hezekiah learned that the Assyrians were planning to attack Jerusalem, he "went up to the house of the Lord and spread it before the Lord" (2 Kings 19:14). Today, some prefer to go to a chapel or church to pray. The atmosphere created by the altar, symbols, and stained-glass windows helps them to feel the presence of God.

Bed. A Psalmist prayed when he was in bed. "When I think of you on my bed, and meditate on you in the watches of the night" (Psalm 63:6). For some praying in bed may be the only time when there is silence and solitude in the home. A problem is falling asleep while praying! Would that be an affront to God?

Open air. Abraham sent his servant to find a wife for Isaac. When the servant arrived at a well in Nahor, he had even his ten camels kneel while he prayed for success in finding the right person for Isaac (Genesis 24:11-14).

Hillside. Jacob was fleeing from the wrath of Esau and when night came he stopped at Bethel, used a stone for a pillow, and had a dream of angels. In the morning he prayed and made promises to God that he tithe (Genesis 28:18-22).

Riverside. Paul and his associates went to preach at Philippi but there was no synagogue in the city. On the sabbath they went to the side of a river and held a prayer meeting there (Acts 16:13).

Seashore. Paul and his company were on their way to Jerusalem. When the ship came to Tyre, the Christians of that area escorted Paul outside the city. "There we knelt down on the beach and prayed" (Acts 21:5).

Private room. Jesus in the Sermon on the Mount taught that a person should go to one's private room, shut the door, and pray (Matthew 6:6).

It is obvious that any and every place can be a place of prayer. One may be better than another. Each person needs to find the best place to be alone with God where, free from distractions and interruptions, a wonderful time can be spent with Christ. St. Augustine insisted upon freedom from interruptions. Ten days before he died, he asked friends to visit him only when his physician came or when food was brought, so that he might spend his whole time in prayer. Once again, it proves that the place of prayer is important if prayer is to be meaningful and effective.

Posture Of Prayer

Our posture reflects our feelings and convictions when we pray. It also helps us to feel the way we want to feel when we pray.

Our head. It is customary to bow the head when we pray. Bowing the head before God acknowledges the holiness and greatness of God. The publican who went to the temple to pray would not lift his head and eyes to heaven because he sensed his unworthiness. A bowed head expresses our humility, our finitude, and our creaturehood before the holy, transcendent, glorious God.

Our eyes. When we pray, we usually close our eyes unless we are reading a prayer. Why do we close our eyes? Why do couples usually close their eyes when they kiss each other? It is such an exciting and meaningful moment! We close our eyes during prayer because we can no more look into the face of God than we can look directly into the sun. God is too brilliant and glorious for human eyes to behold. Moreover, no one has ever seen God, because he is invisible. We can see God only in Christ. Closed eyes in prayer helps us to shut out the world with its distractions. With the world shut out, we can concentrate on what we are saying or on what we hear when we are led in prayer.

Our hands. What do we do or should we do with our hands when we pray? Surely, we do not use our hands when we pray, our lips but not our hands! And that can be a problem. What we do with our hands may detract from prayer. Some put their hands in their pockets and jingle their coins! Women may be fingering their handkerchiefs or reaching into their purses. Usually hands are folded in the front or back of a person. Roman Catholics usually have their hands together and held in front of their chests similar to Albert Durer's famous "praying hands." When a group prays, individuals often hold hands with their neighbors. Holding hands with others while praying solidifies the group before God.

Our bodies. One position of the body in prayer is *kneeling*. St. Paul knelt when he prayed, "I bow my knees before the Father" (Ephesians 3:14). At the end of his farewell message to the Ephesians "he knelt down with them all and prayed." When we kneel we express our humility. We kneel also when we want a favor. On our knees we plead and beseech, for we are desperate for help. Do you remember how you knelt before the girl asking her to marry you, or was this only in the good old days? When we kneel in prayer, we beg for mercy: "Lord, have mercy on me."

We have the example of great Christians who knelt for prayer. Eusebius, a fourth century church historian, tells about James, the brother of Jesus and head of the Jerusalem church: "He (James) used to enter alone in the temple and be found kneeling and praying for forgiveness for the people so that his knees grew hard like a camel's." Look at your knees — are they calloused from kneeling in prayer? Washington was another who knelt. In the early days of our country the British Ambassador visited Congress and asked how he could tell George Washington from the others. "It will be easy," explained the friend. "When the members pray, President Washington is the one who kneels." Are we known for our kneeling? Alice Monroe tells about her mother: "My mother prayed on her knees at midday, at night, and first thing in the morning. Every day opened up to her to have God's will done in it. Every night she totted up what she'd done and said and thought, to see how it squared with Him."

Why don't we kneel in church as much as we used to? The liturgical churches, Roman Catholic, Episcopal, and Lutheran, used to have kneelers in the pews and at the altar rail for kneeling. Does it mean that we no longer need to express our humility before God or need to plead for mercy to have sins forgiven? In a recent tour of Nova Scotia we went to see the largest wooden church in North America, a Roman Catholic church. I searched for a place to kneel but found none. Are we the losers for it? One time a preacher, watching a marble cutter at work, exclaimed, "I wish I could deal such clanging blows on stony hearts!" The sculptor replied, "Maybe you could if you like me worked on your knees."

Standing is another posture for prayer. In prayer Jeremiah said to Yahweh, "Remember how I *stood* before you to speak good for them, to turn your wrath from them?" (Jeremiah 18:20). In the parable Jesus told about two men who went to the temple to pray. Both of them stood for their prayers.

Why stand for prayer? Prayer means we are in the presence of our glorious God. To express our respect and reverence we want to stand. In years past, gentlemen stood when a lady entered the room to express their respect and honor. Whenever the President, regardless of party, comes into a room, all, out of respect for the office of the presidency, stand. Dare we no less do the same when we come into God's presence to present our praise and petitions?

Sitting is a third way of posturing for prayer. King David sat to pray: "Then King David went in and sat before the Lord and said . . ." (2 Samuel 7:18). Sitting expresses equality. When one comes for an interview, one does not sit down until invited to do so. Because of the symbolism of sitting as equality some are unwilling to sit when they pray. On the other hand, sitting enables a person to rest and relax. If you have much to say to God, you may want to sit. It is said that sitting for prayer in non-liturgical churches resulted from long pastoral prayers that extended from Genesis to Revelation.

Prostration is posture for prayer. In Gethsemane Jesus used this posture. In Matthew 26:39 it is reported that Jesus "threw himself on the ground and prayed." This is the posture Moslems use for prayer. They fall on their faces before Allah. As individuals Christian may use this posture but because of practical difficulties with stationary pews, Christians as a whole do not practice it in worship services. Nevertheless it is a worthy way to express to God our total unworthiness to come into his presence.

Reflection/Discussion

1. How much time each day do you set aside for prayer? Are you satisfied with this allotment?

2. Is there a danger in praying too much?

3. Does the place of prayer add or detract from your prayers?

4. If citizens stand when the President enters a room, should we stand for prayer?

5. Should a church make provision for people to kneel other than at a communion rail?

6. Why do we instinctively close our eyes when we pray?

"O Lord, our heavenly Father, almighty and everlasting God, who hast safely brought us to the beginning of this day. Defend us in the same with Thy mighty power and grant that this day we fall into no sin, neither run into any kind of danger; but that all our doings, being ordered by Thy governance, may be righteous in Thy sight; through Jesus Christ, Thy Son, our Lord. Amen."

— Martin Luther

7
The Variety
Of Prayer

Do you think God gets tired of hearing the same content and the same form of our prayers over and over again? The Psalmist cried out, "O sing to the Lord a new song" (Psalm 96:1). Perhaps we should say, "O pray to the Lord a new prayer!" Variety, they say, is the spice of life. It is also the spice of prayer. We tend to say in our prayers the same old thing in the same old way. God must be bored! A variety of prayers is available. Richard J. Foster, in a recent book, *Prayer*, gives 21 different kinds of prayer from "Simple Prayer" to "Radical Prayer."

Variety Of Biblical Prayers

1. Prayer without Faith — read Acts 12:1-17. The prayer group asking for Peter's release from a Jerusalem prison did not believe their prayer would be answered.

2. Prayer of Struggle — read Genesis 32:22-32. All night long Jacob wrestles with God before he faces Esau who, he thinks, is coming to kill him.

3. Prayer of Intensity — read 2 Kings 20:1-7. With tears King Hezekiah prayed for an extension of his life and he got it!

4. Prayer of Intercession — read Genesis 18:22-33. Abraham intercedes for Lot who is in the sin-city of Sodom.

5. Prayer of Friendship — read Exodus 33:7-11. In a prayer tent outside the camp, Moses went daily to commune with his friend, Yahweh. "The Lord used to speak to Moses face to face, as one speaks to a friend" (v. 11).

6. Prayer of Submission — read Matthew 26:36-46. Even the Son of God had to submit to his Father's will to the point of death on a cross.

7. Prayer of Communication — read Genesis 28:10-22. Run-away Jacob communicated with Yahweh in a dream in which he saw angels (messengers) ascending and descending from earth to heaven and from heaven to earth.

8. Prayer of Silence — read 1 Samuel 1:12-14. Though Hannah's lips moved, she prayed silently for a child. Because the high priest, Eli, did not hear her words, he concluded she was drunk.

Meaningless Prayers

One variety of prayers is meaningless prayers. They may just as well be not offered because they do not reach the throne of God. One of these meaningless prayers is Fax prayers. Recently a fax service, run by Bezek the Israeli national phone company, enables Jews from anywhere in the world to have their prayers delivered by Bezek employees to the ancient and holy Wailing Wall in Jerusalem and deposited in the crevices of the wall. Paper prayers cannot speak! To think so is irrational and stupid.

Prayers that are faith-less are meaningless also. Faith is an absolute, indispensable requirement in prayer. There must be faith in God, in a God who hears and answers prayer. Without faith prayers consist of empty words. We are talking to ourselves.

Repetitious prayers are also meaningless. In the Sermon on the Mount Jesus warned his Disciples not to pray like the Gentiles who used empty phrases and repeated endlessly thinking they would be heard for their much praying. God hears the prayer for the first time. He is not hard of hearing that the prayer must be repeated. Repetitious prayer is an exercise in futility. Thousands of "Our Fathers" and "Hail Marys" do not shorten the stay in Purgatory nor do they persuade God to answer the petition.

Silent Prayers

Silent prayers are usually offered by individuals who are praying by themselves. There is no one nearby. So, if that is the case, why speak audibly in prayer? Yet, in our private prayers we do speak but not audibly. Like Hannah, our lips may move but we make no sound. Why do we do that? We need silent words to express our thoughts, petitions, and feelings. You may picture Christ sitting in the chair next to you. You speak to him as you would speak to your dearest friend. It is warm, personal, and intimate. You tell him how much you love him and share your secrets, hopes, and dreams. This makes the prayer too personal to share with other humans. Oswald Chambers wrote, "The real reason for prayer is intimacy of relation with our Father." We may be so depressed and despondent that we do not want anybody to know about it except our merciful God and we say, "Lord Jesus Christ, Son of God, have mercy on me." Or, it may be that we have sins to confess. We see no good reason for others to know about them. We feel free to tell God and know he is so loving that he will forgive.

When as individuals we pray silently, we find it easier to stop talking and give God a chance to talk to us. He does speak when we are still. He often speaks in a small voice like a whisper. Someone called Jeremiah 33:3 the telephone verse of the Bible: "Call to me and I will answer you, and will tell you great and hidden things . . . ." One of the serious missing links in our personal and corporate prayers is silence. Who is more important to do the speaking: God or you? God has some very important things to say to you. He says he loves you, that your sins are forgiven, that heaven is a surety for you, that in the end all things will work for your good. To hear these and even more you and I must listen in our prayer time to God.

The truth is that true prayer needs no oral verbal expression. Prayer is communion and fellowship with God through Christ. In this communion we and God share thoughts and feelings. Something deeper than words is spirit. Our spirits reach out to the Great Spirit. The pinnacle of true prayer is just being in God's presence accompanied by peace, contentment, and joy. Three monks made an annual trip to a holy man. Two of the brothers asked many questions and shared thoughts and dreams, but the third man never said a word. After many visits, the holy man spoke to the silent brother. "Though you come often, you ask me no questions." Smiling the silent one said, "It is enough just to be with you, Father."

Oral Prayers

Oral prayers are used for corporate prayers. There is an assembly of believers who engage in prayer. Not all can pray at this time. There is not enough time to give a group of hundreds to pray one after the other. Feeling incapable and unworthy, some refuse to lead in prayer before a group. The prayer is spoken loudly for everyone to hear and engage in the leader's prayer. The leader should never pray as though he/she were praying privately. It is not "I pray" but "We pray." The public prayer is designed to offer prayer for all sorts and conditions of people, not only for the local group, not only for certain needy individuals, not only for the local church, but for the whole church throughout the world, for the nation and its problems, and for the world with its hunger, poverty, and wars. When corporate prayer is offered, it is not one person praying but the entire group is praying. The leader, liturgist, or pastor is praying on behalf of everyone. Corporate prayer is not for the people to listen to someone praying. Each in the congregation is supposed to pray in the words of the leader. Each is to echo the prayer, to repeat silently what is offered. When this is done, corporate prayer has power. Instead of one person praying, now 100, 300, or 500 are praying the same thing. When one person prays, it is like a single candle burning. In corporate prayer, there are 100, 300, or 500 candles burning. Think of the light 500 candles make in contrast to the one candle! This is in line with Jesus' teaching: "If two of you agree on earth about anything you ask, it will be done for you by my Father in heaven" (Matthew 18:19).

An example of an oral corporate prayer is a *Collect*. It "collects" the truth of a Scripture passage or sums up the truth in the Scripture lessons for a particular day of the Church Year usually in one sentence. Some collects used today come from the ancient period of church history. A collect concerning the church:

> *Most gracious Father, we humbly beseech Thee for Thy holy catholic church. Fill it with all truth, in all peace. Where it is corrupt, purify it; where it is in error, direct it; where anything is amiss, reform it; where it is right, strengthen it; where it is in want, provide for it; where it is divided and rent asunder, heal the breaches thereof, O Thou Holy One of Israel; through Jesus Christ our Lord. Amen.*

Another example of corporate prayer is what the church calls the *Pastoral Prayer* or the *General prayer,* or the *Prayer of the Church.* The prayer is designed to cover all the needs of the people, the church, the nation, and the world. To cover all these needs, the prayer is usually lengthy. The following is from *The Book of Common Prayer:*

> *Almighty God, Father of all mercies, we thine unworthy servants do give thee most humble and hearty thanks for all thy goodness and loving-kindness to us and to all men. We bless thee for our creation, preservation, and all the blessings of this life; but above all for thine inestimable love in the redemption of the world by our Lord Jesus Christ, for the means of grace, and for the hope of glory. And, we beseech thee, give us that due sense of all thy mercies, that our hearts may be unfeignedly thankful; and that we show forth thy praise, not only with our lips, but in our lives, by giving up our selves to thy service, and*

*by walking before thee in holiness and righteousness all
our days; through Jesus Christ our Lord, to whom with
thee and the Holy Ghost, be all honor and glory, world
without end. Amen.*

Participatory Prayer

The personal, silent prayer is, of course, by one person.
The oral, corporate prayers are uttered by a leader, pastor,
or priest. In this corporate prayer the assembled people are
led by a leader and the congregation prays with the leader silently. In participatory prayer there is more than one praying. It may be two leaders or it may be the leader and the
congregation. The people audibly participate in the prayer. It
helps people to realize that they, too, are engaged in the prayer.

A *Bidding Prayer* is offered by two leaders or pastors. Also,
the prayer can be offered by the leader and the response by
the congregation. The "bid" is a petition: "Let us pray *for*
. . ." The response gives the content of the petition. A bidding prayer has been used since ancient times, especially during Lent.

> The bid: *"Let us pray, dearly beloved, for the holy church
> of God, that our Lord God would grant it peace and uni-
> ty, and preserve it throughout the world, keeping it per-
> petually upon the true foundation, Jesus Christ."*

> The petition: *"Almighty and everlasting God, who hast
> revealed thy glory to all nations in Jesus Christ and the
> word of his truth: Keep in safety, we beseech thee, the
> works of thy mercy, that thy church, spread throughout
> all nations, may serve in the confession of thy Name;
> through Jesus Christ, thy Son, our Lord. Amen."*

A *Litany* is a congregational prayer with dialogue between
the liturgist (pastor, priest), and the people. Excerpts from a
Litany:

Pastor: *Lord have mercy upon us.*
    Congregation: *Lord, have mercy upon us.*
Be gracious unto us.
    Help us, good Lord.
From all sin, from all error, from all evil:
    Good Lord, deliver us.

A *General* or *Pastoral Prayer* is offered by the liturgist or pastor with the congregation responding. The pastor concludes each petition with "Lord, in your mercy —" The congregation completes the sentence: "Hear our prayer." This is repeated at the end of each petition. In a less formal way usually in non-liturgical churches the people may respond as the prayer proceeds by exclaiming, "Yes, Lord" or "Praise the Lord" or "Thank you, Jesus."

The people should always respond to a leader's prayer with an "Amen" meaning "Yes, so be it." The "Amen" gives the people's affirmation to the leader's petitions as to say "They are our petitions, too, Lord." The "Amen" closes a prayer with confidence, conviction, and assurance that God hears and will answer His people's requests.

Reflection/Discussion

1. Are there any "meaningless" prayers offered in your church?

2. What can anyone do to get a variety of prayers in a church?

3. Can one adequately pray without saying the words of our thoughts directed toward God?

4. Does silence play any part in personal or congregational prayers?

5. How do you feel about read prayers or impromptu or extemporaneous prayers?

6. Does including all sorts and conditions of people here and everywhere make a prayer too long in this modern age?

"Lord, I give up all my own plans and purposes, all my own desires and hopes and accept Thy will for my life. I give myself, my life, my all utterly to Thee to be Thine forever. Fill me and seal me with Thy Holy Spirit. Use me as Thou wilt, send me where Thou wilt, work out Thy whole will in my life at any cost now and forever. Amen."

— Betty Scott Stam

8

The Agony
Of Prayer

I know of two contrasting pictures of Jesus' praying in Gethsemane. One is a picture of poise and peace. Hoffmann's "Christ in Gethsemane" shows Jesus kneeling before a large rock and looking calmly to heaven. The other is a picture I took in the Garden of Gethsemane of a statue of Jesus carved into a stone wall along a pathway. In this picture Jesus is on his knees, his body draped over a large stone, his hands clasped over his head, and his head buried in his outstretched arms. It is a picture of stress, strain, and agony as he struggles with his Father over living and dying.

Some people have the idea that prayer is calm and easy, as an unknown author wrote: "Prayer is so simple. It is like quietly opening a door. And slipping into the very presence of God." For some prayer is a laughing matter. Abraham Lincoln once told of two Quaker women who were discussing the Civil War. One said, "I think Jefferson Davis will win." The other asked, "Why do you think so?" "Because," the first lady explained, "Jefferson is a praying man." "And so is Abraham a praying man." "Yes, but the Lord will think Abraham is joking."

Indeed, prayer is no laughing matter. Prayer can be associated with struggle and wrestling. There is an agony of prayer. It can be a matter of sweat, tears, and blood. It is the Gethsemane side of prayer. It is this side of prayer we will consider at this time.

The Testimony Of Great Pray-ers

The following great Christians witnessed to the agony of prayer:

81

Paul — "I appeal to you, brothers and sisters, by our Lord Jesus Christ and by the love of the Spirit, to join me in *earnest* prayer to God on my behalf" (NRSV).

The RSV puts it: "to *strive* together with me in your prayers to God ..." (Romans 15:30).

Luther — "Nor is prayer ever heard more abundantly than in such *agony* and groaning of a struggling faith." The most powerful prayer is "prayed with *sobs* and *tears*." Luther described Gethsemane as "God struggling with God."

Kierkegaard — "True prayer is a *struggle* with God, in which one triumphs through the triumph of God."

P. T. Forsyth — "To feed the soul we must *toil* at prayer."

From these masters in prayer we learn that prayer can be a striving, struggling, groaning, and toiling event.

Causes Of Prayer Agony

Why does prayer at times have to be one of agony, struggle, and groaning? Consider these reasons:

First, a cause of agony is the desperate situations we are facing at the time. One of these desperate situations is the threat of disaster and destruction. It is not only when or if we are in a desperate situation but also when a member of our family or friend is in that kind of a situation. Abraham had that experience (Genesis 18:22-33) when his nephew was living in Sodom which was so wicked that God planned to obliterate it. If he did, innocent Lot and his family would also be destroyed. Abraham prayed persistently until he received God's assurance that if there were only 10 righteous people in the city, he would not destroy it.

How would we pray if we were threatened with disaster? Suppose we were in the path of a hurricane or tornado, or were in a crossfire between two rival gangs in a city ghetto, or kidnapped and threatened with rape or murder? Suppose a grizzly bear came after us while we were visiting a national park. Would we strive with God in prayer to be saved?

Second, the agony of prayer may be caused by approaching death. King Hezekiah had this experience (Isaiah 38:1-6). Through the prophet Isaiah God told the king he should get his things in order, for he would soon die. Hezekiah would not accept death. He prayed bitterly to be allowed to live. Because of his fervent prayers with tears, God gave him 15 more years of life. Suppose we received a message like that, what would we do? Suppose your doctor told you that you had an inoperable cancer and at best you had only six months to live. Suppose you had to have a heart transplant and the possibility of success was doubtful. Would you agonize in prayer because you wanted to live forever? Perhaps in your prayer you would accuse God of not being fair to you by taking your life prematurely. You may hate God for it. You struggled and wrestled with God until you came to the point of accepting your approaching death. Then you could say, "It is well with my soul. I have peace from surrendering to your will, O God."

Third, the agony of prayer may be the result of disappointment. Hannah was a sorely disappointed wife because she was childless (1 Samuel 1:1-20). Elkanah's other wife, Penninah, had sons and daughters and thereby felt more blessed than Hannah. She became so sad that she would not eat. She was deeply distressed and with tears prayed with all her heart. With agony she prayed until she became pregnant with Samuel.

In our disappointments we, too, may pray in agony. We may have hopes and dreams for our future but they all seem to have ended in ashes. One may have hope of going to college, but the death of a father made it necessary to drop out of school to go to work to support the family. One may have a beautiful dream of a happy marriage with children and a Christian home, but a spouse turns to alcoholism or to another man or woman. One may dream of having a long life but tragedy brings the end when you are only in your 20s. In times like these, when your soul is bitter and distressed, you cry out to God in prayer.

Fourth, fear may cause us to strive with God in prayer. It was so with Jacob who feared to meet his brother, Esau, who was coming with 400 horsemen. Jacob feared that his evil past was catching up with him. The night before Esau was due, Jacob spent the night alone with God with whom he wrestled. Jacob struggled with God until he gained God's blessing (Genesis 32:22-32).

Fear can paralyze us and we flee to God for relief. In our time much fear prevails in our society. There is the fear of violence. We are actually afraid to walk the city streets alone by day or by night. We are not safe even in our homes. Some time ago a man entered a home where children had a slumber party and a 12-year-old girl was kidnapped, raped, and murdered. In this day when companies are reducing their work forces, many people live in fear of losing their jobs and thereby facing unemployment and all the deprivations associated with it. In fears like this, we go to God in prayer seeking safety and security.

Fifth, the agony of prayer may be caused by a conflict between our will and God's will. Jesus' prayer in Gethsemane (Matthew 26:36-46) was one of agony. He told his three Disciples, "I am deeply grieved even to death." His threefold prayer was so strenuous that it caused him to sweat which fell to the ground like drops of blood. Jesus was fighting for his life and was trying to get his Father to see it his way: "My Father, if it be possible, let this cup pass from me."

Each of us may have from time to time a period like Gethsemane. We want something but it is not God's will for us to have it. One of the most difficult things to say is "Thy will be done."

Sixth, prayer becomes a struggle filled with agony of soul when we are deep in despair. A Psalmist (Psalm 130:1) had this experience. From the depth of his being, he prayed, "Out of the depths I cry to you, O Lord. Lord, hear my voice." Life can get that way. All doors seem to be closed to us. We see no sense in going on. All hope has been lost. We are in the cellar of our lives and cry out for light and reason to keep on going when all seems to be lost.

84

Components Of Agonizing Prayer

The Intensity Of Our Desire

If what we pray for or about means little or nothing to us, we will not pray with intensity. Then it does not matter one way or another if the prayer is granted. On the other hand, if it does matter, we will be bold enough to argue, protest, and bargain with God.

In 1540 Luther's good friend, Frederick Myconius, became deathly sick. He himself expected to die within a short time. One night with trembling hand he wrote a fond farewell to Luther whom he loved very much. When Luther received the letter, he immediately sent back the following reply: "I command you in the name of God to live because I still need you in the work of reforming the church. The Lord will never let me hear that you are dead, but will permit you to survive me. For this I am praying, this is my will, and may my will be done, because I seek only to glorify the name of God." If Luther did not care whether Myconius lived or died, if he did not feel the need of Myconius in the work of the Reformation, he would not have prayed with the total intensity of his whole being.

The intensity of our desire in prayer is expressed by our persistence. We will not give up. We want what we want so badly that we will break down the door to God's favor. Abraham kept praying time after time for Lot's deliverance from Sodom. Jacob prayed all night for God's blessing of protection from his brother. Jesus prayed for his life not once but three times. If we mean business about our need, we will never give up praying. Our intensity shows itself physically. With Jesus it will be expressed in sweat or in tears of need. The author of Hebrews gives this description of Gethsemane: "In the days of his flesh, Jesus offered up prayers and supplications with *loud cries and tears* ..." (Hebrews 5:7).

Conforming To God's Will

There is a natural conflict between God's will and the human will. We are by nature willful and selfish. We come into the world as egomaniacs. We are self-centered and our whole world revolves around the "I" — it is what I want, where I want to go or do. To conform the human will to God's will causes strife, struggling, and suffering. It is extremely painful at times. Did you ever witness the taming of a wild horse to where the horse would wear a bridle and tolerate a harness? A horse is useless if he kicks over the traces of his harness, refuses to obey the commands of the driver, and runs away with the wagon until a crash occurs. My father was a dairyman who had a number of milk wagons pulled by horses. When he needed more horses, he bought at a reduced price wild horses shipped from the West. The problem then was to tame the horse to be obedient and to pull the wagon. As a child I was horrified to see how the wild horse was whipped into submission to my father's will. I thought I could not stand to see the horse treated so badly. It was hard for me to realize that was necessary. The horse's will had to be broken to conform to my father's will. Otherwise the horse was of no practical use. It is the same way with our human wills which, with much suffering and discipline, must be brought in line with God's will or we will be of no earthly good to God.

Another way of understanding this is in terms of tuning up a musical instrument. When a youth I tried to play a violin. One thing I learned is that four strings had to be in tune for a harmonious melody. In tuning a string, it had to be stretched almost to the breaking point. The string was under such stress until it gave the right sound. It is that way in getting the strings of our wills to be in perfect harmony with God's will. There will be no sweet music until the human strings give the proper tune matching the perfect tune of God. But, that involves tension, stress on the human part — the agony of getting in tune with God by prayer.

This applies also to a child's and a parent's will. A child is born with a self-centered will opposed to God's will. There is no more self-centered person in the world than a child. The child is naturally interested only in me and mine. The will of a child must be disciplined to conform to the parent's will. The authority of the parent must be acknowledged and accepted. The parent has the right to say to a child, "As long as you live in our house, you are expected to live by our rules and standards of conduct." This calls for obedience which must be learned by discipline. A willful child is usually a spoiled child and a spoiled child is a shame and disgrace to a parent.

The stronger the will of a person results in the stronger resistence to God's or the parent's will. If we are weak and easygoing, there is no problem. If we do not object or resent being told what to say or do, we easily give in to a higher will whether it is the will of God or a spouse or a boss. If we have a will of our own, it becomes agony to make our will God's will.

How then are we to pray? We must always pray "not my will but thine be done." If we pray, "If it be your will to heal," of course it is God's will for us to have health. "If it is your will for me to live," of course God wants us to live and live abundantly. "If it is your will to have peace," of course God wants peace on earth. "If it is your will to change a person," of course God wills godliness and goodness to possess every person. One thing is sure: God's will for us is always good. God loves each of us and desires only the very best for us. Therefore, we pray always to know and do God's will, and to do it we pray for strength, courage, and patience.

To Pray Aright

We may struggle in our prayers because we want to pray aright, but are not sure what to pray that is right. We face questions like these when we turn to pray:

Shall I forgive a wrong or not?
Shall I take the low or the high road?
Do I want success at any price?
Shall I take the easy or hard way out?

What we pray for or about depends in determining the will of God for our lives. Shall I divorce or put up with a miserable married life? What shall I do with my life? What does God want me to do with my life? Is this the right person for me to marry? Shall I go to college or get a job? Do we want to have a family? To get the right answer for these and other questions may require much stress and strain culminating in the agony of prayer.

Results Of The Agony

When we are struggling or striving with God in prayer, there are certain things we must do. One is persistence. It is vital that we keep up the struggle with God. Another is patience. It may take time for God to answer our prayer and time for our situation to change. God has eternity to work out our problems and God is never in a hurry. With patience we have faith God will take care of the needs we prayed about. Add submission to praying with agony. When we are able to say, "Your will be done," we experience peace, a peace that passes our understanding. Though the struggle with God is strenuous, we will in the end receive God's comfort. When Jesus accepted God's will for him to go to the cross, the Record tells us, "Then an angel from heaven appeared to him and gave him strength" (Luke 22:43).

We conclude with the wise words of Hartley Coleridge:

Be not afraid to pray — to pray is right,
Pray, if thou canst, with hope; but ever pray,
Though hope be weak, or sick with long delay;
Pray in the darkness; if there be no light.

88

Reflection/Discussion

1. How do you explain Luther's description of Jesus' prayer in Gethsemane: "God struggling with God"?

2. Why must prayer be a struggle or must it be?

3. Is it possible for one to know the mind of Christ?

4. How can we pray to do the will of God if we do not know his will?

5. In the struggle with God, can a human win?

6. Can one always say "Your will be done"? Is everything God's will?

"O God, from whom all holy desires, all good counsels, and all just works do proceed: Give unto Thy servants that peace which the world cannot give; that our hearts may be set to obey Thy commandments, and also that by Thee, we, being defended from the fear of our enemies, may pass our time in rest and quietness, through the merits of Jesus Christ our Savior. Amen."

— Martin Luther

9

Prayer In
Personal Devotions

In today's society the world is too much with us. It is a world of materialism and secularism. The American people have been feeding on the media. The average American watches TV seven hours a day. And what do they see? Much of it is garbage telling about violence, sex, greed, adultery, and crime.

As a result, people are looking for spirituality, something or someone higher than the mundane. In his recent book, *Prayer,* Richard Foster claims, "The scandal of Christianity in our day is the heresy of a five percent spirituality." Feeling that the church is not meeting this longing for spirituality, many are turning to the cults, New Age, Yoga, Transcendental Meditation, and others.

One answer to fulfilling this need is the worship of the church. But, the hour of worship is not enough to give adequate spiritual formation. It calls for one hour per week in God's presence. There are 168 hours in the week to deal with the world, the flesh, and the devil. Moreover, if everyone went to church, it would not be so bad. How many are in church on a Sunday? A recent study indicated only 20 percent of Protestants and 28 percent of Roman Catholics attend worship, a drop from Gallup's poll of 45 percent of Protestants and 51 percent of Roman Catholics. In addition, are worshippers getting spiritually fed? In some churches, the people are cold with unfriendliness, the sermon is deadly dull, and the music is off key. Recently a professor of theology in a Chicago seminary announced that he no longer attends chapel services because he feels worse for attending. Many claim that going to worship is a waste of time and effort.

The result is that many are spiritually impoverished. They are running their lives on empty. Life for them is cold and barren. There seems to be no reason to live. They have learned that man cannot live by bread alone. There must be something more than eating, sleeping, and going to work. Is there no perpendicular dimension to life? As a result we have little or no inner strength and we are in danger of collapsing from within. When the Statue of Liberty was remodeled a few years ago, it was discovered that the entire inside support system had to be replaced. The outside copper skin of the statue was in good condition but the inner iron supports had rusted and corroded. It was estimated that if nothing was done, in 20 years the statue would have fallen over. Similarly, the great "unsinkable" Titanic sank not because an iceberg in the Atlantic put a big gash in her side, but the problem, discovered after extensive sea-bottom photos, was that the ship's steel plating was brittle. A small impact caused major cracks in her side: that took the mighty ship to the bottom of the ocean. We as persons and people are in danger of the same tragedy. Without inner spiritual strength we will collapse from the pressure of our materialistic, godless society.

A Tryst With God

While corporate worship is important and indispensable for spiritual maturity, it needs to be supplemented by the individual's care of the soul. This calls for a daily tryst with God when we have intimate fellowship with him. In this tryst, we meet with God, sense his presence, and as friends we talk with him and he with us.

What does one do in this tryst? What does one say or does one say anything to Almighty God? When and where does the meeting take place? How long should it last? You may be saying, "I've never tried it. No one has ever taught me what to do or say."

How long should this tryst last? It varies with each person, from a few minutes to a few hours. Martin Luther spent three hours and John Wesley two hours each day for personal devotions. We wonder how they ever found that much time to give to prayer and what they did in those hours. The time they spent with God each day explains how they became some of the greatest religious leaders the world has ever known. Their time with God was the secret of their success and their productivity. How much time can you give to developing your relationship with God? We live such busy lives that we wonder where we would get the time. We all have more to do than the time allows. It comes down to taking time for devotions. This calls for determining the priorities of life. How important is a relationship with God? Is it worth 10 minutes or a half hour, or even a whole hour spent with God?

If we decide we are going to give time each day for devotions, when should we hold this tryst? Of course, the time of day varies according to one's schedule and work. It may be different for a mother with small children or a business man going to work at seven a.m., or a senior citizen with no specific appointments. It is generally agreed that if it is possible, the morning is the best time to be alone with God. When does an orchestra tune up — before, after, or during the concert? Morning devotions is getting in tune with God at the beginning of the day and then the rest of the day is lived in the presence of God. The tryst affects your spirit and attitude for the entire day. You get the day started right. Moreover, in the morning you are more able to concentrate in your prayer. The questions, problems, and needs that occur later in the day have not yet appeared and therefore do not distract you in your prayers.

Where is the best place for these devotions? It should be the same place every day, a kind of hide-away. It needs to be a place that is comfortable, free from distractions and interruptions, and where you can relax. A religious picture or symbol can help to create an atmosphere of prayer. John Wesley had a little prayer room just off his bedroom. In this little room was a chair for him to read the Bible and a prayer desk for kneeling in prayer. After a while, this place becomes like a shrine associated with times spent with God.

A Procedure For Devotions

Suppose you never had a tryst with God. You may then wonder about the procedure. How does one begin? What does one say, if anything? A suggested procedure follows:

Shut The Door

We have this directive from Jesus himself: "Whenever you pray, go into your room and *shut the door* ..." (Matthew 6:6). He tells us to shut the door of our prayer room. We are not just to enter a room, but upon entering to shut the door. You are saying, "Private. Stay out!" This includes members of the family and friends. You want to be alone with God. You want no interruptions nor distractions. The family, spouse and children need to cooperate in this and it may be very difficult to get them to comply with your wish.

We shut the door to have solitude. This means we want to be alone with God, and like the Disciples at the Transfiguration, we want to see no one except Jesus only. This may be difficult for some who are afraid to be alone. They keep from being by themselves by listening to radio or TV, or by having someone always near for conversation. When they are alone, fears and worries come to mind. Bad experiences are re-lived. They cannot be at peace with themselves because of a bad conscience. They try to keep busy and so occupied that they will have no time to think about themselves.

If we are alone with God, we are with our best friend. We have his undivided attention. His Spirit can drive out all negative thoughts and fears.

Also, we shut the door to our room of prayer that we can have silence. We shut out the noise from the family's talk as well as the noises outside the house. Someone said, "Silence is the only voice of God." We demand silence when we want to hear or accomplish something important. Silence is demanded in a library in order to concentrate on reading. When we go to a concert, there must be silence or the orchestra will not begin. It is said that Arturo Toscanini insisted on silence to the degree that he had programs printed on velvet paper to prevent the noise of turning the pages. In a tennis match, a player waits for quiet before he/she serves the ball. When a golfer is on a tee, his partners will not dare to whisper lest they distract him from hitting a hole in one! In church we are called to be silent: "The Lord is in his holy temple; let all the earth keep silence before him" (Habbakuk 2:20). Elijah learned that God speaks in a still, small voice. To hear his voice we must be silent.

Take Off Your Shoes

This may not be difficult to do, for many take off their shoes when they enter home. "Take off your shoes" is not meant literally. It is a symbolic action. Taking off our shoes is an act of reverence. When Yahweh came to Moses at the burning bush that did not burn up, he said, "Remove the sandals from your feet, for the place on which you are standing is holy ground" (Exodus 3:5). At the time Moses was in a meadow caring for his sheep. Why would it be holy ground? It was holy because God was there, and wherever he is, the place or article becomes holy whether it is a building, book, or sacrament. When we enter a room for devotions, God comes to meet us. He is truly present, and the room becomes holy. It means that we must realize God is present and we need to be reverent.

The taking off of our shoes means taking off our sins. Sandals or shoes are related to the dirt of the streets. God is a holy, righteous God and cannot tolerate the dirt of sin. To remove our shoes is to get rid of our sin in the presence of

God. For this reason, a worship service usually begins with a confession of sins in order that the people coming from a sinful world may be spiritually cleansed. There follows the Introit meaning that now being cleansed of our sin we may introit, enter in, to the presence of our holy God. Sin separates us from God. Before we can have rapport with him, feel close to him, we must get right with God through our confession and his forgiveness.

Open The Window

Daniel prayed three times a day before an open window (Daniel 6:10). It was a way of saying that he was open to his God. When we pray, we need to open the window of our prayer room, for we need to be open and receptive to what God would say and give us. If we are not open in mind and heart, God cannot bless us. He will not knock down the door to get to us. He will not shout to get us to hear him. He will not force himself on us. If we have a closed mind and think that we have all the answers, God cannot help us.

Unless we are open and receptive, we will not recognize the presence of God nor will we hear his voice. Do you recall the story of Baalam and his ass? Baalam was called by a king to come and curse the Israelites on their way to the Promised Land. On his donkey he started on his way to the king. On the way an angel came with drawn sword and blocked the way. Baalam did not see the angel and brutally beat his donkey for not going ahead. Finally the donkey spoke to Baalam in Baalam's own language. The ass had more sight and sensitivity to God than Baalam did. Unless we have a receptive spirit with open eyes, ears, and heart, we will not see nor hear God when we are at our daily devotions.

Fold your hands

When you have devotions what do you do with your hands? What you do with them reveals the condition of your heart. Do you wring your hands? If so, it shows you are worried. Do you spread your hands? You are saying you are in despair. Do you close your hands in a fist? You are angry and combative. The proper thing is to fold your hands. It signifies you are relaxed and at peace with yourself and God.

With folded hands you are relaxed. You are not afraid to be with God, for you know he loves you. You are not worried about your job, school, or family, because you know God will take care of them for you. In your relaxation, pour out your heart to him. Tell him how good he is. Adore, praise, and thank him for his blessings.

A Format For Devotions

You are in your prayer room. You have shut the door, taken off your shoes, opened the window, and you sit with folded hands. Now what? What are you going to say or do?

Read The Scriptures

In our personal devotions, we are there to listen to God. He speaks to us in his Word, the Bible. Before we can say anything to him in prayer, we want to get a message from him concerning our lives. Thus, we begin our devotions by reading the Bible.

But, why read the Bible? What is the purpose? Is it a duty or an obligation? We read the Bible for instruction. It informs and educates us about God, life, and ourselves. We learn the nature and the will of God. He instructs us about the meaning of life. In the Bible, like no other book, we get the whole truth about spiritual matters.

We also read the Bible for information. Who are we? Where did we come from? Who made the world and us? We want to know how God revealed himself through the ages. How poor we would be if we did not know about the lives and doings of the patriarchs and prophets. Our ultimate source of information about Jesus and the first Christians is the Bible.

Read the Bible for inspiration. The Scriptures are saturated with the Holy Spirit. When we read it, we receive the Spirit who inspires us to seek that which is above. The Word and the Spirit are inseparable. George Mueller says it truly: "The Spirit and the Word must be combined. If I look to the Spirit alone without the Word, I lay myself open to great delusions. If the Holy Spirit guides us at all, he will do it according to the Scriptures and never contrary to them."

If you are a beginner in reading the Bible, you may ask what to read and where to start. Each day open your devotions with a Psalm. This will get you acclimated to the Spirit and lead you to spiritual thoughts. Try one of these: Psalms 1, 8, 19, 90, 91, 121, 146, 150. Then read a chapter from the Old Testament where you will become acquainted with the mighty acts of God. Now turn to the New Testament and read the old story of Jesus and his love.

Every Christian should read the Bible from cover to cover at least once in a lifetime. Martin Luther read it three times each year. If you read three chapters on weekdays and five on Sundays, you will finish the entire Bible in a year to the very day you started. John Wesley was a Bible reader. Explaining his daily devotions, he said, "I sit down alone. Only God is here. In his presence I open and read this book." "This book" was the Bible. He was a man of one book.

Think

To think is not easy and not everybody does it. Someone said that 75 percent of the people do not think, 15 percent think they think, but only 10 percent think. It is not enough to read the Bible and at once close the book and go your way without another thought. Think about what you read. Reflect and meditate upon it. Meditate — what is that? It is serious and deep thinking. Ask yourself what the Word is in the words you just read. What is the truth revealed here? What is God saying to you in this passage? Think of what the truth is in relation to your life. How does it apply to you?

In the passage you just read, seek guidance in God's Word. Look for answers in the passage to these basic questions:

Is there any command for me to obey?
Is there any promise for me to claim?
Is there any example for me to follow?
Is there any sin for me to confess?
Is there any prayer for me to echo?

Not all these questions are answered in every passage. How many can you find in Matthew 17:1-8?

Pray

Having read the Word and thought about it, you are ready to pray. God has spoken to you. What is your response? Does the passage call for a confession of sin or faith? Do you have reason to thank and praise God? Does God promise blessings that you need? In *Life Together* Dietrich Bonhoeffer wrote, "The most promising method of prayer is to allow oneself to be guided by the word of the Scriptures, to pray on the basis of a word of Scripture. Prayer means nothing but the readiness and willingness to receive and appropriate the Word."

Grow

After prayer related to the Word, it is very helpful to read enrichment material for your growth in spirituality. One may choose to read a sermon a day. As an apple a day is supposed to keep the doctor away, a sermon a day may keep the devil away! Sermons by Harry Emerson Fosdick, George Buttrick, Peter Marshall, David H.C. Reid, and James Stewart are good for the soul. You might read a chapter a day from books like Oswald Chambers' *My Utmost For The Highest,* Brother

Lawrence's *Practicing The Presence Of God,* and Dietrich Bonhoeffer's *The Cost Of Discipleship* and *Life Together.* The books by Henri Nouwen and Thomas Merton are usually very helpful in gaining spiritual strength.

Reflection/Discussion

1. Is it necessary to have a stated time for devotions? Why can't I have my prayer time while on a walk or driving to work?

2. What obstacles must be faced to have daily devotions?

3. Is there such a thing as a dry time for the soul?

4. Is it possible to have a quiet time with God even though there is no privacy or silence?

5. How can you get the family to leave you alone for a devotional period?

6. Can one hear God speak apart from the Bible?

"Most gracious Father, we humbly beseech Thee for Thy holy catholic church. Fill it with all truth, in peace. Where it is corrupt, purify it; where it is in error, direct it; where anything is amiss, reform it; where it is right, strengthen and confirm it; where it is in want, provide for it; where it is divided and rent asunder, heal the breaches thereof, O Thou Holy One of Israel; through Jesus Christ our Lord. Amen."

— Archbishop William Laud

10
Prayer
And Healing

What does prayer have to do with healing? Does it really work? Let the experience of one man answer. Lewis Grizzard, a popular syndicated columnist of Atlanta's *Constitution,* for the third time had a heart valve replacement at Emory University Hospital. He wrote, "I spent days sticking one foot in and out of death's door." After the operation doctors and nurses told him, "We exhausted all medical possibilities. We did everything we knew to do for you, and it probably wouldn't have been enough. What saved you was prayer." Grizzard continued, "Can you believe that? Great men and women saying such a thing in 1993? If the medical experts say prayer brought me back from certain death, who am I to doubt them?" Obviously and convincingly prayer does have something to do with healing.

A Theology Of Healing

Since the Clinton administration came into office, Americans are excited about doing something about health care. The cost has soared to a trillion dollars annually. Yet, 37 million Americans are without health insurance.

God is far more concerned about the health of people than is President Clinton. The Bible teaches that God is on the side of healing. He cares as much about the health of our bodies as about our souls. God's will is for us to be strong and healthy. He made us that way and wants us to remain that way. Sickness is the work of Satan, of his destructive powers. When we pray for health, we have an approving God who wants us to recover. God's only Son was and is a healer. He is known as the Great Physician. Speaking of God, Frederick Buechner once wrote, "You do not have to persuade him to heal. You do not have to ask him to change his mind and be merciful instead of indifferent. You ask God to use your prayer as a channel through which the healing power of his love can flow into whatever body or soul you pray for" (*The Magnificent Defeat,* p. 128).

Therefore, when we pray we should not say, "Heal me if it is your will." It is always God's will for us to have life with health in body, mind, and spirit. For some unknown reason, God's will may be frustrated and the prayer is not answered affirmatively. In that case, God is also disappointed and suffers with us. The ultimate healing we can get is death when we are united with Christ in heaven where there is no more pain nor sorrow.

In this theology of healing is an understanding of the nature of a person. A human is an indivisible unity of body, mind, and soul. Each is not a separate, independent unit existing in a water-tight compartment. Consider this diagram:

A Person or Self

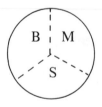

Note that the lines separating the units are not solid but dotted. This is to indicate that the one affects the other. Modern medicine tries to treat the whole person. It is sometimes called psychosomatic or holistic medicine when the whole person is treated. Often the staff includes a physician, a psychologist, and a pastor.

A positive attitude of one unit promotes health of the whole person. A Psalmist said, "Being cheerful keeps you healthy.

104

It is slow death to be gloomy all the time" (Psalm 7:22). Norman Cousins in his book, *Anatomy Of Illness*, tells how humor brought about his recovery. Elizabeth Barrett Browning was an invalid for 39 years, but recovered when she fell in love with Robert Browning. This love inspired her to write the classic love poems, *Sonnets From The Portuguese.*

A negative attitude can cause ill-health. One Sunday a preacher was very negative about life. He was down on everything and everyone. In the congregation was his physician. At the close of the service, the doctor said to a friend, "Well, after that sermon, I see that I'll have to have the pastor come in for a check-up. His liver is acting up again." We all know from experience that when we are fatigued, malnourished, or out of sleep, we get blue, despondent, and critical. The body affects the mind and spirit just as the mind and spirit can affect the condition of the body.

Where does prayer fit into health? It is said that 60 percent of all patients who visit physicians' offices could cure themselves if they got rid of their fears and worries. A noted theologian of yesteryear said, "The sovereign cure for worry is prayer." Prayer deals with the soul. It puts us in relationship with God. God is life, health, and peace of mind and soul. A healthy soul, one with a harmonious relationship with God, contributes to the health of body and mind.

Mahatma Gandhi had this to say about prayer: "I discovered that after a time of prayer, I was able to do far greater amounts of work. A doctor has testified as a medical fact that my blood pressure was lowered by it, my nerves calmer, my mind rested and alert, my whole body in better health. I was refreshed and ready for work, and if previously I had been in a mood of pessimism and despair after I prayed I was charged with new hope and confidence."

Dr. Herbert Benson, Harvard Medical School cardiologist, maintains, "Prayer can lower blood pressure, alleviate pain and stress, and bring about peace of mind. Patients who recited prayers were successful at lowering metabolic rates, slowing the heart rate, and reducing other symptoms of stress."

The Biblical Meaning Of Healing

According to Scripture, to heal is to be made whole. Holy and whole belong together. A holy person is a whole person. A whole person is a healthy person. The Greek word to heal or save is variously translated. In Mark 10:52 Jesus says to blind Bartimaeus: "Thy faith hath made thee whole" (KJV), "Your faith has made you well" (NRSV), "Your faith has healed you" (NIV). "Whole" is used by Gaither in his hymn, "He Touched Me": "He touched me and made me whole."

The lack of wholeness means brokenness, separation, estrangement, schism, dysfunction, and sickness. By healing Jesus makes us whole. It means taking the parts of us that are separated and binding us into a unified whole. It is atonement, at-one-ment. Jesus makes us whole in each area of our being:

Physical: Mark 10:52 — Bartimaeus was not whole. Sight was missing.

Mental: Mark 5:9 — Jesus brought the many faceted psyche of the Gadarene Demoniac to a unity of mind. He told Jesus, "My name is Legion, for we are many."

Spiritual: John 17:21 — In his high priestly prayer, Jesus asked his Father for unity. "As you, Father, are in me and I am in you, may they also be in us."

In 1993 the nation learned of a broken person. Katherine Power attended Brandeis University, was a straight A student, and the pride and joy of her family. As a student she joined anti-Viet Nam protestors. While holding up a bank, one of her party shot a policeman. For 23 years she was on the FBI's most wanted list. Katherine changed her name to Alice Metzinger, married, had a son, and was a successful restauranteur. After 23 years she decided to turn herself in. She received a jail sentence of eight years. Her husband explained why she turned herself in, "She wants to be *whole*." She was two persons living a lie. She wanted to be one whole person, Katherine Power.

Sin And Sickness

In the Bible sin and sickness are related. It teaches that not all sickness is due to sin. The classic example is Job. He was a righteous, godly man who perfectly obeyed the Law. Then disaster, death, and tragedy came. Four friends came to Job and tried to comfort him by trying to persuade him that his sin caused the misfortune. He fought back and insisted upon his innocence. Why does a righteous man suffer? The answer is not sin.

Jesus taught that sin is not necessarily the cause of illness. One day the Disciples saw a man blind from birth. They asked, "Rabbi, who sinned, this man or his parents, that he was born blind?" Jesus explained, "Neither this man nor his parents sinned" (John 9:1-3).

On the other hand, sin can cause sickness. Smoking can cause lung cancer. Excessive use of alcohol can result in cirrhosis of the liver. AIDS can follow homosexual sexual relations and/or dirty drug needles. The media reports daily the rapes, murders, and violence resulting from immoral ways of life.

Sickness and sin are often combined in the Scriptures. Jesus writes, "Therefore confess your *sins* to one another, and pray for one another, so that you may be *healed*" (James 5:16).

When a paralytic man was let down through a roof in order to be in Jesus' presence, Jesus said to him, "Your sins are forgiven" (Matthew 9:2-8). What does physical paralysis have to do with forgiveness of sins? There is a similar connection in Psalm 103:3: "Who forgives all your iniquity, who heals all your diseases." The connection is probably due to the fact that when the soul is healed by forgiveness, the body and mind are healed at the same time. This takes us back to the unity of a person consisting of body, mind, and soul. What affects one affects another at the same time.

The Church And Healing

Healing is not limited to the church. In the Old Testament there are many miracles of healing. Prayer was the means of healing.

1 Kings 17:17-24 — Elijah revives a widow's son through prayer.

2 Kings 4:32-37 — Elisha raises the son of a Shunamanite woman by prayer.

2 Kings 20:1-7 — King Hezekiah prays for healing and gets 15 more years of life.

Psalm 30:2 — "O Lord my God, I cried for you to help, and you have healed me."

Jesus had a ministry of healing. Matthew 4:23 mentions the threefold ministry of Jesus: preaching, teaching, and healing. He also used prayer in his healing. Before calling Lazarus out of his tomb, Jesus prayed — John 11:41-42.

The church was commissioned to heal in addition to teaching and preaching. In Matthew 10:1 we read that Jesus sent his Disciples "to cure every disease and every sickness." Healing is an essential function of the church. The Disciples healed many according to Acts 5:16. Peter raised Dorcas from death — "Then he knelt down and prayed" (Acts 9:40-42). Paul also engaged in healing. Read how Paul healed a cripple — Acts 14:8-10.

The church today continues her healing ministry. It is not only physical healing but also emotional, mental, psychological, and spiritual healing. Worship is a healing experience by bringing us into the presence of God. It is healing to thank and praise God. One feels better when one hears the Word of God and meets fellow-worshippers. Preaching the Gospel is also a healing function. A gospel sermon inspires, encourages, and gives hope. The church carries on her healing ministry by visiting and praying for the sick. Some churches have special healing services each week. The Sacraments bring us God's grace which heals our wounded souls with merciful forgiveness.

Biblical Basis For Healing

One of the main passages upon which the church's healing ministry is based is James 5:13-16:

Verse 13 — Sufferers should pray for relief. More people have burdens and problems than we may realize. One woman reports that her marriage of 29 years is ending. Her 19-year-old daughter is lost in alcohol, other drugs, and sex. Her older daughter, newly married, now relates more closely to her husband than to her. Friends have been sick. Loved ones were lost. Her father has a terminal illness. Sin, illness, and death hover around. James urges her to turn to prayer.

Verse 14 — Elders of the church are to pray for the sick. Ministers are ordained as elders. They are supposed to be super-Christians living close to God and dedicated to God's service. Why the elders? Why not anybody? In verse 16 James writes, "The prayer of the righteous is powerful and effective." An elder is supposed to be closer to God and more righteous. Therefore, the prayers of elders are expected to be more effective.

Verse 14 — Anoint with oil in the name of Jesus. It is not a mere anointing with oil but oil in the name of Jesus. It is related to him as a healing agent.

Verse 15 — The prayer of faith will save (heal) the sick and sins will be forgiven. Again, we see the connection of sin and sickness with forgiveness as a healing agent.

Verse 16 — Healing comes from confessing sins to each other and from praying for each other.

The church has a Biblical basis for her healing ministry and she is called to fulfill her mandate.

Methods Of Healing

1. Pray — sincerely, fervently, and confidently in full faith.
2. Touch by the laying on of hands. Jesus healed by touching the patient and laying his hands on him/her. One case: healing a blind man at Bethsaida by both touching and by the laying on of hands (Mark 8:22-23).
3. Anoint with oil. In the Bible oil was used for the anointing of kings and high priests. It was also used for healing.

Oil softened the wound; the Good Samaritan poured oil in the wounds of the afflicted Jew. Oil was a medical ointment. The Disciples used oil in healing: "They drove out many demons and rubbed olive oil on many sick people and healed them" (Mark 6:13).

How To Pray For Healing For Others

1. Listen with compassion to the sick person.
2. Ask God boldly and confidently for healing doubting nothing.
3. Touch or lay your hands on the sick.
4. If possible and practical, anoint with oil.
5. Persist in praying. Healing is not always immediate. Jesus prayed twice before a blind man received his sight (Mark 8:22-26).
6. See Christ in the sick. pray with Mother Teresa: "Dearest Lord, may I see you today and every day in the person of your sick and whilst nursing them minister unto you. Though you hide yourself behind the unattractive disguise of the irritable, the exacting, the unreasonable, may I still recognize you and say, 'Jesus, my patient, how sweet it is to serve you.' O beloved sick, how doubly dear you are to me when you personify Christ and what a privilege is mine to be allowed to tend you ...."

How To Pray For Healing For Self

1. Desire to be healed. Be open and receptive. Long to be well. Jesus asks, "Do you want to be made well?" (John 5:6).
2. Have faith in the power and willingness of God to heal you. Have complete confidence in his power and grace.
3. Be grateful for what God has done and for what he will do for you. Think health. Will recovery. Expect to feel better.

4. Give God reasons for wanting to regain health:
Work you still need to do for God.
A person you still need to win for Christ.
Dependents who need you to provide for them.

Practical Considerations

1. Should one pray for incurable illnesses?

There are diseases that presently are incurable: cancer, arthritis, AIDS, crippled bones, et al. Are we to accept the condition in a hopeless and helpless attitude? Should we pray on in the belief that with God all things are possible? In 1992 a wife and mother discovered she had breast cancer with tumors in her liver and bones. In 1985 a tumor was found in her left breast and she had it surgically removed. For seven years she was given the all-clear report. Now there was a tumor in her liver. Chemotherapy was the treatment, but the best they could do was to reduce it but not eliminate it. Her family, friends, and church began to pray for a cure. In 1993 a CT scan revealed that the liver tumor was no longer present. Prayer was the answer.

If there is no hope for recovery, we can still pray. We can pray for the patient's comfort and courage in facing difficult days ahead and the end of life. We can pray that the sick person will grow in faith as preparation for eternity.

2. Why does God heal some but not all?

It is apparent that God does not heal all even though fervent prayers were offered for the recovery of health. It may be due to the lack of faith, for in Nazareth Jesus could not cure illnesses because of the people's lack of faith. Also, maybe there was no healing because it was not God's will. Paul had this experience when he prayed for the removal of the thorn in his flesh. God said, "My grace is sufficient for you."

The answer is that nobody knows why some are healed and others are not. Our responsibility is to pray for all and for any condition. Let God decide who is to be healed. Whatever God decides will be good for all concerned.

3. Should we rely *solely* on prayer for healing?

Unfortunately some do. In the past year a boy died in a diabetic coma without medical treatment while his mother, a Christian Scientist, prayed. Her church taught that physical illness and injury can be treated through prayer alone. A Minneapolis jury ordered the Christian Science Church to pay punitive damages of $9 million.

Likewise, a two-year-old girl with sickle cell anemia in St. Petersburg was critically ill. Her mother, a Jehovah's Witness, refused to permit her daughter to receive a blood transfusion. Jehovah's Witnesses claim that certain Biblical passages forbid blood transfusions. A court judge ordered the little girl to have the transfusion regardless of her mother's opposition.

On the other hand, should we rely solely on medical science for healing? Some do, but Christians do not. They use both medical science and prayer for healing. God usually works through medical science, but God is not limited to human ingenuity. The ideal is to combine medicine and prayer.

Reflection/Discussion

1. Is there a time to stop asking for healing?
2. Is sin the cause of sickness?
3. Are there sources of healing other than prayer?
4. Should we pray for the incurable? If so, how and for what should we pray?
5. Is it proper to pray, "If it is your will"?
6. Is all healing instantaneous?

"Teach us, good Lord,
to serve you as you deserve;
to give and not to count the cost;
to fight and not to heed the wounds;
to toil and not to seek for rest;
to labor and not to ask for any reward,
save that of knowing that we do your will,
Through Jesus Christ our Lord. Amen."
— Ignatius Loyola

11
Praying In
The Spirit

Have you ever thought of prayer as a demonic force for evil? David T. Jenkins raises this question when he writes: "Prayer as such is not necessarily a good thing. Unless it is directed to the right Person in a way He has laid down, it can become a demonic force and do untold damage to man and nation. It can be a highly dangerous thing, the most subtle and effective means of hiding man from the face of God" (*Prayer And The Service Of God*, pp. 17, 34).

Indeed, prayer can be a demonic force. Prayer is used by Satanists and by witches and others to impose or cancel curses on people. It is misused and abused when prayer is used to get God on our side rather than putting ourselves on God's side. It is an abuse of prayer to use it to get God to do our will rather than for us to do God's will. Prayer can be used to get God on human terms rather than our meeting God's terms. We can pray selfishly and even pray for harm to come to an enemy.

It depends upon the spirit possessing us when we pray. One spirit has us pray to get what we want. Another spirit leads us to pray to know what God wants for us. Does an evil spirit or the Holy Spirit dominate our prayers? From common personal experience we know that usually we do or say things according to the spirit we feel at the time. We don't write a long overdue letter because we do not feel like writing. We refuse to go to a party because we are not in a party spirit. When a wife asks her husband to clean out the basement, he fails to do it because he is not in the mood for it. When Sunday morning comes and someone says, "Let's go to church," with the wrong spirit we say, "Aw, do I have to go? I am not in the mood to go today." It is the same with prayer. If we have no spirit, we neglect our prayers. If the wrong spirit possesses us, we will pray amiss. To pray like Jesus we must pray in the Holy Spirit.

The Holy Spirit And Prayer

Paul directs us to "pray in the Spirit at all times" (Ephesians 6:18). Jude also commands, "Pray in the Holy Spirit" (Jude 20). The Holy Spirit provides the basis for Christian prayer. We cannot pray without the Spirit.

The Spirit enables us to call God "Father." When we pray, we pray as children to our heavenly Father. "When we cry 'Abba! Father!' it is that very Spirit bearing witness with our spirit that we are children of God" (Romans 8:15-16). If we pray to Christ as our Lord, the Spirit enables us to call upon him as "Lord." "No one can say 'Jesus is Lord' except by the Holy Spirit" (1 Corinthians 12:3). When we pray about spiritual truths, it is the Spirit that gives us an understanding of spiritual realities. Without the Spirit, we would pray about things in a way that we would be talking about things we know nothing about. Paul writes, "So also no one comprehends what is truly God's except the Spirit of God" (1 Corinthians 2:11).

To pray in the Spirit requires that we possess the Holy Spirit. That is basic and elemental. How could anyone pray in the Spirit if the Spirit were not present in the person praying? Therefore, we need to ask, "Do we have the Holy Spirit? If not, how does one acquire the Spirit?"

The Spirit comes in answer to prayer. Jesus promised, "How much more will the heavenly Father give the Holy Spirit to those who ask him!" (Luke 11:13). Prayer brought the Spirit to the Disciples at Pentecost. After Jesus' ascension, they went to Jerusalem and prayed for 10 days for the promised Spirit to come, and he did! Today some churches prepare for a revival by holding 24-hour prayer vigils prior to the first service of the series.

A second way the Spirit comes to us is in and through the Word of God. This Word is recorded in the Scriptures which were written by writers possessed by the Spirit. Therefore, the Word and Spirit are inseparable. Luther taught, "God will not give you his Spirit without the external Word." The "external Word" is the Bible. The Spirit produced the Bible which is saturated with the Spirit. The Bible is like a sponge saturated with water. Take the sponge out of the water and wherever you squeeze it, water drops out. It is the same with the Scriptures. Touch it and use it and the Spirit comes to you.

The Word comes in various forms. There is the read Word when we read the Bible. Philip, returning from Jerusalem, found the Ethiopian eunuch reading the Bible. The eunuch asked him to explain what he was reading. When he understood, he asked Philip why he could not be baptized (Acts 8:26-39). An intelligent reading of the Bible brings to the reader a measure of the Spirit.

The Word can also come by hearing it taught, preached, or individually witnessed. Peter was invited by Cornelius, a Roman officer, to come to his house to tell him and his friends about the Gospel. Peter came and preached Christ. As he was preaching "the Holy Spirit fell upon all who heard the Word" (Acts 10:44). In order that people can receive the Holy Spirit, the Bible is taught in the church school and preached from the pulpits. Week by week the Holy Spirit is replenished in the hearers.

A third way the Word brings us the Spirit is by its visible means, the Sacraments of the church. A Sacrament is the Word accompanied by a visible sign. In a sacrament you can see the Word and through the Word the Spirit comes. It happened to Jesus when he was baptized. The Spirit came to him like a dove alighting upon him. "And just as he was coming up out of the water, he saw the heavens torn apart and the Spirit descending like a dove on him" (Mark 1:10).

In addition to the Word, the Holy Spirit can come to us by the laying on of hands. When Paul came to Ephesus, he asked them whether they had received the Holy Spirit. They did not know there was a Holy Spirit. Paul then baptized them in the name of Jesus and "when Paul laid his hands upon them, the Holy Spirit came upon them" (Acts 19:6). The church still uses this method of bringing the Spirit. At baptisms, confirmations, and ordinations hands are laid upon the candidates that they might receive the Holy Spirit.

To pray in the Spirit is to pray to the triune God. Christians pray to the Holy Spirit through Jesus to God the Father. We pray in God (Spirit) through God (Christ) to God the Father. We pray to the Spirit who is in us. In the Spirit we pray to Christ who is our mediator with God the Father, the wholly other One.

The Spirit's Part In Prayer

When we pray in the Spirit, he helps us to pray as we ought. How does he do this? First, he guides us to the truth. Jesus taught, "When the Spirit of truth comes, he will guide you into all the truth" (John 16:13). The Spirit of God is the truth of God. When we pray in the Spirit, we will pray the truth as recorded in the Scriptures. We will not deal with falsehood or heresy. We will be praying the truth about God, life, and salvation.

Second, the Holy Spirit is a teacher. Jesus said, "But, the Advocate, the Holy Spirit, whom the Father will send in my name, will teach you everything" (John 14:26). Since we do not know how to pray as we ought (Romans 8:26), the Holy Spirit comes to our rescue. He tells us what to pray for and how to pray.

Third, the Holy Spirit intercedes for us with the Father God. In Romans 8:26-27 Paul assures us that the Spirit intercedes for the saints. We sinners need someone to speak in our behalf, to appeal to the mercy of God. We have no excuse. We have no merit for God to be good to us. The Spirit, God's own spirit of love, pleads for us. He secures the Father's grace for us. We are weak in our prayers. We often ask foolishly.

118

But, the Spirit intercedes and makes all things right with God for us.

Fourth, the Holy Spirit gives the right spirit for prayer. In Galatians 5:22 Paul lists nine fruits of the Spirit. If we are going to pray aright, we must have the right spirit and attitude. In the parable of the Pharisee and Publican at prayer, Jesus taught that humility is necessary to get prayers answered. When in prayer we address a holy, righteous God, we need a spirit of reverence as held by Isaiah when he was worshipping in the temple and saw God seated on a high throne and heard angels singing, "Holy, Holy, Holy." Since God is love and he commands us to love him and our neighbor, we can only properly pray when our hearts are filled with love. You and I cannot pray effectively if we hate or are angry with someone. Add the spirit of faith and trust to our prayers. We need to pray with full faith and confidence that God is, that he hears and answers prayer, that he cares for us and will help us. Such faith and confidence was expressed in one of Luther's prayers: "Lord God, heavenly Father, I pray and I will not be denied. The answer should and must be Yes and Amen, and nothing else. Trusting in the consolation of Thy fathomable grace, and not in my own righteousness, I kneel before Thee and pray ...."

Praying With The Heart

Praying in the Spirit is praying with the heart. "Heart" stands for feeling and emotion. It is praying in the spirit of love. This calls for praying with warmth, sincerity, and depth of feeling. It is not praying from the top of our heads but from the bottom of our hearts. It is not what the mind knows but what the heart feels. Often the heart understands what the mind cannot grasp. We know in our hearts the love we have but we are unable to describe or explain what the heart feels.

Praying with the heart may result in a loss of words. Paul had this experience: "that very Spirit intercedes with sighs *too deep for words"* (Romans 8:26). The love we have is more than words. When we want to praise and glorify God, to tell him how grateful we are, words seem to be totally inadequate. Our elation in being one with him and our souls' well-being cannot be adequately expressed. The best we can do is sigh.

Praying with the heart may result in what is called "prayer language." It is not the same as "speaking in tongues" but it is akin to it. A person gets so caught up in the emotion of praying that the person speaks a special language known only to the one praying.

Glossolalia is a result of praying with the heart. "Glosso" means "tongue" and "lalia" constitutes "languages." Glossolalia, therefore, is a tongue language. It was a problem in the Corinthian church. In chapters 12 and 14 of 1 Corinthians Paul discusses it. In a state of spiritual ecstasy and emotionalism, a person prays in a language unknown to the person praying and to those hearing the prayer. It is for the pray-er's edification, an expression of an intense religious experience. Though Paul tells us he spoke in tongues, he gives his position in 1 Corinthians 14:19 — "In church I would rather speak five words with my mind, in order to instruct others also, than 10,000 words in a tongue." Speaking in tongues may edify the speaker but it does not help the listeners simply because the language is unintelligible. This type of speaking must not be confused with the Pentecost experience when each Disciple spoke in a foreign language so that the various nationalities in Jerusalem would hear the Gospel in their own language. To overcome the problem of people not being able to understand tongue-speaking, Paul urged that an interpreter should be present.

To this day there are some who speak in tongues in worship services. It is not to be condemned but understood as an expression of extreme emotionalism. It is most meaningful to the person speaking in tongues as proof of having the Spirit. However, it is an individual matter and not helpful to the congregation.

There are certain disadvantages to speaking in tongues:

1. Often it disrupts a worship service. Glossolalia cannot be scheduled. The worship service may lose decency and order.

2. Glossolalia may result in pride on the part of those who speak in tongues. They can be proud of their gift of the Spirit and of their ability to speak in unknown tongues. "I can do something you can't do!" Pride is a violation of the Spirit.

3. Glossolalia may lead to despising others who cannot speak in tongues. Speakers in tongues may look down on others as "second class" Christians.

4. This spirit of pride may cause a division in the church. The congregation may split into charismatics and non-charismatics. Pity the pastor who is caught in the middle!

5. The expressions of the tongue-speakers may be offensive to those worshippers who relish dignity, reverence, and order in the worship services. The clapping, raised hands and arms, the cries of "Praise the Lord" and "Amen," and shouting may turn people off and drive them out of the church.

Praying With The Mind

Paul taught that we should pray in the Spirit, with the heart but also with the mind. "I will pray with the Spirit, but I will pray with the mind also" (1 Corinthians 14:15). If we do not pray with the mind, we may be praying with the wrong spirit. To prevent this we need to use reason. An aged archbishop once said to a young clergyman: "Two things can save the world, prayer and thought. But the trouble is that the people who think do not pray and the people who pray do not think." In addition to reason, we can safeguard our prayers from the wrong spirit by revelation found in the Scriptures.

Just as we are commanded to love God with all our hearts, we are to love God with all our minds. This applies to prayer: think and then pray. The mind gives structure to our prayers. What should we pray for and in what order? Our minds tell us we need to pray with adoration, confession, thanksgiving, and supplication. How much time should be spent on each one? Are the prayers all-inclusive: personal, community, church, nation, world concerns?

Praying with the mind will keep us from repetition and from using pat words. Today a popular word is *just* "God, I *just* wanted to talk to you. I was *just* wondering whether you'd think about giving me *just* a bit more than yesterday. I really don't deserve it, but you're *just* a little bigger than me, so I *just* don't think it would put you out too much if you *just* noticed little me *just* a little while. And I *just* want to thank you for listening for *just* this time" (Martin E. Marty).

To pray with the mind enables us to plan what to say, what to request, how to say it. Does the prayer harmonize with God's will? Prayer calls for previous thought and planning. Accordingly, it is unfair to call upon a person without notice to lead in public prayer. Some pastors spend as much time preparing the pastoral prayer as they do preparing their sermons. Think! Don't let yourself repeat yourself. Keep your mind from wandering and going off on tangents. Pray and think; think and pray!

How To Pray In The Spirit

Here are some simple steps to take in learning how to pray in the Spirit:

Cultivate The Spirit

At baptism you probably received the initial gift of the Holy Spirit. That Spirit needs to be fed and cultivated throughout life. No one, except Jesus, was ever "full of the Spirit." We can never get enough of the Spirit. We must grow in Him. The Spirit in us is cultivated by prayer, worship, Bible reading, Christian service and fellowship.

Begin Your Prayer By Invoking The Holy Spirit.

Hymns may help to feel and possess the Spirit:

"Come, Holy Spirit, our souls inspire,
Enlighten with celestial fire"

or

"Spirit of the living God, Fall fresh on me.
Melt me, mold me, fill me, use me.
Spirit of the living God, fall fresh on me."

or

"Breathe on me, O breath of God
Till I am wholly thine,
Till every earthly part of me
Glows with thy fire divine."

Relax And Rest To Let The Spirit Come To You.

The Spirit cannot be commanded or forced. He comes to the person who is receptive and relaxed.

Let The Spirit Move On Your Heart.

He will give you thoughts and words to express those thoughts.

A Case Study In Spirit Praying: Luke 2:22-35

The Occasion For The Prayer

Jewish law at the time of the Holy Family required a mother to be ritually cleansed of childbirth 40 days after giving birth. The child was to be presented to the Lord with an appropriate gift as a thankoffering. Mary and Joseph traveled four miles from Bethlehem to Jerusalem to the temple for the presentation. Today the church observes this event 40 days after Christmas and it is known as the "Presentation of the Lord."

Simeon, an aged devout man, was promised by God that he would not die until he saw the Messiah for whom he prayed and longed for. When the parents brought the baby Jesus into the temple, Simeon recognized the Messiah in the baby and broke out in a song known today as the "Nunc Dimittis" still sung today in many churches.

The Spirit's Work

Simeon was the product of the Spirit. He was given the Spirit — "The Holy Spirit rested on him" (v. 25). The Spirit revealed to him that he would see the Christ before he died (v. 26). Simeon was guided by the Spirit to meet the baby Jesus in the temple and enabled Simeon to recognize the Messiah in the child. "Guided by the Spirit" (v. 27) Simeon took the baby in his arms and praised God, "Lord, now you are dismissing your servant in peace ..." (v. 29).

The Spirit's Gifts

The Spirit gave vision to Simeon. In Jesus he saw the Lord's salvation (v. 30).

The Spirit gave Simeon an understanding of the universal Savior (v. 32).

The Spirit caused Simeon to praise God for the revelation and gift (v. 32).

Reflection/Discussion

1. Do you accept or reject the claim that prayer can be a demonic force?

2. In what or whose spirit can we pray?

3. What does the Bible have to do with the Holy Spirit?

4. Is our inability to pray due to our lack of Spirit?

5. If speaking in tongues is an expression of the Holy Spirit, should not all Christians have this ability?

6. How do you react to Paul's statement, "In church I would rather speak five words with my mind in order to instruct others also, than 10,000 words in a tongue"?

"O God, who hast made of one blood all nations of men, mercifully receive the prayers that we offer for our anxious and troubled world. Send Thy light into our darkness, and guide the nations as one family into the ways of peace. Take away all prejudice and hatred and fear. Strengthen in us day by day the will to understand. And to those, who by their counsels lead the people of the earth, grant a right judgment, that so through them and us Thy will be done; through Jesus Christ our Lord. Amen."

— William Barclay

12

The Power
Of Prayer

We are living in a power age. We use power tools from toothbrushes to screwdrivers. Jet planes on take-off thunder with power. Our autos are driven by 200 horsepower engines. Day after day we use power machines, but do we offer prayers of power?

Would you be interested in prayer if you knew that prayer has the power to make you the kind of person God intends you to be and do? Would you use prayer as the power to rise above your environment, to do the seemingly impossible tasks, and to make your life count for good? It is true that we kneel in weakness but we rise in strength. Someone truly said, "More things are wrought by prayer than this world dreams of."

Demonstrations Of Prayer Power

It is one thing to claim there is power in prayer. It is another to give specific, concrete demonstrations of that power. Would you believe that prayer can cause the place of prayer to shake? When Peter and John were released by the Jerusalem authorities, their friends prayed with thanks and praise. In Acts 4:31 we read, "When they had prayed, the place in which they were gathered together was shaken." The prayer room vibrated and trembled with power. Now, is that power or not?

Do you think prayer has the power to affect the planets? In Joshua 10:12-14 we learn that Joshua leads the Israelites in a battle with the Amorites. He prayed that the sun and moon stand still until the Israelites won the battle. "There has been no day like it before or since, when the Lord heeded a human voice" (v. 14).

Suppose you were a married woman and found yourself to be barren. For years you tried to have a child, but nothing happened. Would you believe that a prayer for a child would result in your pregnancy? It happened to a woman named Hannah. You can read about her experience in 1 Samuel 1:3-20. With tears she prayed for a baby. Her prayer was answered with a son, Samuel. For her, prayer had the power of fertility.

Do you think prayer has the power to revive a dead person? In the Old Testament there is the story of Elijah and the death of the son of a widow of Zarephath. Read 1 Kings 17:17-24. In great grief she goes to Elijah who prays three times for the child. He prayed, "O Lord my God, let this child's life come into him again" (v. 21). The Lord listened to the voice of Elijah and the child revived (v. 22). A similar situation can be found in the New Testament — Acts 9:36-43. A devout disciple, Dorcas, known for the clothes she made for the poor, died. The church called Peter to come. Upon arrival he knelt down and prayed. After she opened her eyes and sat up, Peter showed her to be alive.

Suppose you went to your physician for a medical checkup. He found a malignancy and said you probably had only a few weeks to live. You were shocked. You could not believe it. You wanted to live. You had important things to do before you died. Would you think of praying for an extension of life? King Hezekiah got the bad news he would die soon. He turned to God and wept bitterly. He begged for a longer life. God heard his prayer and gave him 15 more years. See 2 Kings 20:1-7.

Prayer has the power to get you out of an illicit love affair with a married man. In a letter to Ann Landers, the woman explains: "I was addicted to a married man who was poison. I called him on the phone at leave five times a day. If he wasn't where he said he would be, I'd go crazy. I knew I had to break up with him, because he was taking over my life day and night. It was like being enslaved. I tried acupuncture, hypnosis, meditation, and biofeedback. Nothing worked. Then one day I spotted a shiny silver object on the sidewalk. It was a little lapel

pin that said, 'Try God.' I picked it up and thought to myself, why not? I've tried everything else. I hope you won't think
I'm some kind of a nut, Ann, but after a week of deep prayer
I suddenly didn't want to see my married lover ever again. I
don't know what anyone else would call it, and I really don't
care. To me it was a miracle."

Prayer has the power to even turn away an enemy. In the
mountains of Tennessee there was a preacher who spoke against
the town bully, Burt Lynch. Burt planned to get even with the
preacher by beating him up. One day they met and Burt was
about to attack the preacher. Before the fight started, the
preacher asked Burt if he could pray first. The request was
granted. The preacher fell on his knees and began to pray. "O
Lord, I do not want to hurt Burt. You remember what happened to others I fought. One had his nose broken. Another
had two black eyes. Another received a broken arm. And forgive me, Lord, for knocking one man out." When the preacher
said, "Amen," he looked up but Burt was not there. In the
distance was a cloud of dust caused by Burt's frantic escape.

Prayer is the secret to a successful church. One of the
greatest preachers of the 19th century was Spurgeon in Lon-
don. One day a visitor came to Spurgeon's tabernacle and asked
a man who happened to be Spurgeon if he could see the power plant of the church. He took the visitor to the basement
of the church where the stranger thought he would see huge
equipment which operated the building. When Spurgeon
opened the door, there were 700 people on their knees praying for the church services. Then Spurgeon explained, "This
is our power plant."

Witnesses To Prayer Power

We have seen evidences of the power of prayer. Now let
us hear what people say about prayer's power.

Suppose you were 90 years old and your husband was 100.
Someone told you that next year this time you would have a

child. How would you react? Would you laugh or cry? This occurred with Abraham and Sarah (Genesis 18:1-15). Sarah laughed at the angels' message. One of the angels said, "Is anything too hard for the Lord?" Well, is there anything that God cannot do?

Hear the testimony of Jesus regarding the power of prayer. In Matthew 7:7 Jesus taught, "Ask and it will be given you." There were no exceptions nor limitations. Just ask and you will have it! Look up Matthew 19:26. Here Jesus says, "With God all things are possible." Not a few things, not some things, but all things are possible through prayer. Take a look at John 16:23 where Jesus says, "Whatsoever you shall ask the Father in my name, he will give it to you." "Whatsoever" covers everything. A similar statement is in Matthew 21:22 — "All things whatsoever you shall ask in prayer, believing, you shall receive." Here again Jesus uses "all things" and "whatsoever." There is no limit to the power of prayer. We must note, however, that all things are for the asking with two conditions: "believing" and "in my name." Not anyone nor everyone gets what is asked for. To receive the request there must be faith in Jesus and the prayer must harmonize with the Spirit and will of Christ.

Paul believed in the power of prayer. In Ephesians 3:20 he wrote: "Now to him who by the power at work within us is able to do far more abundantly than all that we ask or think ..." God is able to do more for us through prayer than we can possibly ask or think.

Chrysostom, the golden-tongued preacher of the early church, is the patron saint of preachers. He witnessed: "There is nothing more powerful than prayer, and there is nothing to be compared with it."

J. Edgar Hoover, for many years head of the FBI, had this to say about the power of prayer: "Prayer is man's greatest means of tapping the infinite resources of God." In other words, through prayer we can draw upon the power of God to meet our needs.

Alexis Carrel, a distinguished Christian medical scientist, gives his witness to prayer: "Prayer is the most powerful form of energy one can generate. The influence of prayer on the human mind and body is as demonstrable as that of secreting glands. Prayer is a force as real as territorial gravity. It supplies us with a steady flow of sustaining power in our daily lives."

Prayer's Source Of Power

We have been considering "the power of prayer." Have you been saying that the power is in prayer? Does the act of praying produce miracles? No, it is not prayer that has the power. Prayer is only the means of power. The only source of power is the triune God, Father, Son, and Holy Spirit.

Power comes from God the Father, for he is the Creator and his work is creation. At times we get a glimpse of his power in natural events. The people caught in Hurricane Andrew will never forget the power that caused damage in the billions. Think of the power of a tornado that wipes out an entire town. An earthquake brings death and destruction to hundreds of thousands. A raging flood can wash away hundreds of homes. The power of God the Father in natural events is just the tip of the iceberg of God's almighty, omnipotent power.

The power of prayer comes also from God the Son. Before his ascension he told his Disciples, "All power is given unto me in heaven and in earth" (KJV). At another time he promised, "And I, if I be lifted up, will draw all men to me." He is our Redeemer and his work is redemption. The most difficult work is not in creating the universe but in creating new people. Jesus' power was demonstrated on the cross when he saved all humankind from death and hell. And what is the nature of his power? It is the power of love. There is no greater power. A country veterinarian was called to a farm where a cow was stuck in the mud. He gave the cow a shot of medicine, rubbed its tail with two sticks, and poured water in her ears. Nothing worked. The cow had given up. Ten men, a horse, and a tractor could not pull her out of the hole. Then the vet got an idea. He had the cow's calf brought to the scene. The calf made a cry for help. Instantly the cow heaved and splashed out of the mire. Human effort and knowledge could not do the job, but love did, love of a cow for her calf! It is the love of Christ that saves us from the mud of sin.

God the Holy Spirit is identified with power. Jesus told the Disciples, "You will receive power when the Holy Spirit has come upon you" (Acts 1: 8). Because the Holy Spirit is God, the third person of the Trinity, the Holy Spirit has the very power of God. When we pray in the Spirit, we receive the very power of God to be and do what God commands.

The Place Of Prayer In God's Power

Prayer communicates with God and connects us with God. To live is to be touched of God. To get in touch with God means we get connected with the source of God's spiritual power. Are you old enough to remember the trolley cars that used to run on our city streets? If you do, you will remember that at the rear of the trolley was a pole with a little wheel on the end. The conductor would go out and let the pole go up and connect with the electricity cable. Then the trolley could run because it was empowered by electricity. Now prayer is like that pole which touches the electric cable. The power of God flows into the one who prays.

A frail little lady, past 70 years of age, continued to work as a seamstress. A friend once asked her, "How do you manage to work so hard and steadily?" She explained, "I'm like a street car before it is connected with the power wire. Upon rising in the morning, I connect with power from on high. I pray and put my hand in the Savior's hand. I feel the power of the Spirit passing into me. Then I go on and do what I have to do."

Again, prayer can be likened to the Alaskan pipeline that carries oil from the north to the south of Alaska. In that pipeline flows millions of gallons of oil that helps to drive our cars and oil our manufacturing machinery. It is the channel or means of bringing the power of oil to civilization. Our help comes from the Lord. He is the source of our strength and health. Prayer is the pipeline that brings divine sustenance to us.

Now we face a problem. We have been talking about prayer in terms of an individual who contacts God for him/herself. That is all well and good, but what about intercessory prayer? The one for whom we pray may not pray. How then can the power of God come to this person? Oswald Chambers claims, "What happens when saints pray is that the power of the Almighty is brought to bear on the one for whom they are praying."

It is possible for intercessory prayer to bring the power of God upon people who may not pray for themselves. Prayer is not a physical or mechanical contact with God. It is a spiritual condition and transaction. This makes prayer effective on others for whom we pray. Jesus in Gethsemane asked his men to pray for him. Often Paul wrote, "Pray for me that I might preach the gospel boldly." Dr. Nels Ferre tells about hearing of a Southern Baptist minister who was being severely criticized for his theological and social views. Ferre never met the man but started to pray for him and sent him a card to encourage him. Some years later, when Ferre was teaching at Oxford, Mississippi, the door bell rang and the Baptist preacher stood there. He said, "I had to come by to thank you. I had gotten to the place of a nervous breakdown. My wife and I decided we had to quit the ministry. I went to the mailbox and there was your card. God wiped the windshield clean. And I started all over again."

Are there limits to God's power through prayer? Although God is all-powerful and prayer taps that power, there are limits to our praying for power.

For one thing, we should never ask God to go against his nature in order to answer our prayers. Regardless of our prayers, no matter how often or how intensely we pray, God cannot go against his nature of truth and grace. God cannot deny himself. God limits himself to his own laws.

Moreover , we dare not ask God to use his power to make people cooperate in answering our prayers. Sometimes God must wait for people to cooperate with him to answer our petitions. In our prayers we cannot expect God to force people to cooperate. This may result in the fact that God's will can be frustrated. He wants to help and bless us; he wants to answer our prayers. But, if the persons involved are stubborn and resist God, there is nothing God can do about it.

A third limit to our prayers for power is asking God to change things so that we may be blessed. One often hears or sees a plaque saying, "Prayer Changes Things." That is not true! Prayer does not change things. Prayer changes people and people change things. God works internally and not externally by force. His love changes us in our minds and hearts. With a new heart, the person makes external changes in his/her way of life. A six-year-old boy was helping his dad in the garden. While his father was digging, the boy picked up a daffodil bud and sat down to explore it. He pulled the bud apart and tried to make it a full flower. The result was a mess. Frustrated he called, "Daddy, why can't I open the bud into a flower? How does God open it into a beautiful flower?" Before his dad could answer, he said, "Oh, I know, God always works from the inside." It is as the great philosopher-theologian Soren Kierkegaard said, "Prayer does not change God but changes him who prays."

Prayer And Power Failure

When there is a physical power failure, we are in trouble. There is no electricity to give us light, heat our water, cook our food, or cool/heat our homes. Is it possible that in our prayers we at times experience a prayer-power failure? Why is this so? Is it because God is not able or not willing to answer our prayer?

Consider the case in Matthew 8:1-3. When Jesus came down from the mountain where he preached the "Sermon on the Mount," accompanied by a crowd, a leper came and knelt before him. In his prayer the leper said, "Lord, if you choose, you can make me clean." Jesus replied, "I do choose. Be made clean!" The leper knew Jesus had the ability to heal even an incurable disease, but was he willing? Here Jesus shows he was both able and willing to answer the leper's prayer. The two must go together if a prayer is to be answered. One can be able but not willing or one can be willing but not able to help. When a prayer is not answered, is it a case of God not being willing or able? The episode of Jesus and the leper proves that God is both willing and able to help us.

Why then do we not sometimes receive the power that comes through prayer? For instance, a German company recently distributed blood tainted with the HIV virus, and now thousands upon thousands are terrified that they innocently will get AIDS and certain death. Probably many will pray for a cure, but at this time there is no medical cure. Why does God not answer the prayer of these people? Is he not willing or able?

This issue is a personal concern. I have a granddaughter who is confined to a state hospital. Her parents have taken her from specialist to specialist, from hospital to hospital. No one can say what causes Karen to lose self-control to the extent that she becomes violent, so violent that her parents can hardly subdue her. Because they could not control her, they had to place her in a public institution. For most of her 27 years, she has been in a home or hospital. I pray for her daily asking God to touch her body and mind that she might live a normal life. I face the same question: Is God not willing or not able to help?

We do not know the answer. What can we do until an answer to our prayer comes? First, we can keep faith in God and not surrender to skepticism or bitterness. Keep faith in the goodness and mercy of God. Second, keep on praying for recovery in the hope that in the future there will be a change or there will be a medical discovery that will solve the problem. Third, with God's help, make the most of a bad situation.

Claim God's grace to carry on patiently and heroically. One day a World War veteran with a leg shot off appeared at a shrine where miracles of healing took place. As he hobbled up to the shrine, someone remarked, "That silly man! Does he think God will give him back his leg?" The veteran overheard the remark and answered, "Of course I do not expect God to give me back my leg. But I am going to pray for God to help me to live without it."

Are we using all of God's power for our needs? A small boy was trying to move a big rock and was unable to lift it. His father saw the situation and asked, "Are you using all your strength?" "Yes, I am," the boy replied impatiently. "No," the father replied, "you are not. You haven't asked me to help." Our heavenly Father would love to help move the immovable roadblocks in our lives, but have we asked him for help?

Reflection/Discussion

1. Is there any limit to God's power?
2. Does prayer change things or people?
3. God may be able but is he always willing to answer prayer?
4. Is the power in prayer or in God?
5. Does the power of prayer apply also to those for whom we pray?
6. Does all prayer have power?

"O Lord, support us all the day long until the evening comes and the busy world is hushed and the fever of life is over and our work is done. Then in Thy mercy grant us a safe lodging and a holy rest and peace at the last through Jesus Christ our Lord. Amen."

— John Henry Cardinal Newman

13

The Perfect Prayer

The Lord's Prayer is the perfect prayer. It is the best of the best prayers whether in or out of the Bible. There is none better from A to Z: Abraham to Zechariah. The prayer reflects the pray-er, the Lord. He was the perfect person who had a oneness with God — "The Father and I are one" (John 10:30).

The perfect prayer is short and simple. Jesus practiced his teaching: "Do not heap up empty phrases as the Gentiles do; for they think that they will be heard because of their many words" (Matthew 6:7). In the traditional version of the Lord's Prayer there are only 55 words. In the contemporary version there are five less words. What can you say in only 50 words? Every word therefore must be packed with meaning. The contents are comprehensive covering all our needs as well as praise and thanks. The prayer covers concerns for God: his name, kingdom, and will. Also, it covers our human needs: food, forgiveness, strength, and courage. All of this is done in a simple, easy, childlike fashion that speaks to the youngest as well as the oldest pray-er.

Because it is the perfect prayer, it has never been or ever will be surpassed. Columnist Sydney Harris tried, in a prayer titled, "A Lord's Prayer for our Time":

> *Our parent who is everywhere in the cosmos, we honor you today and every day; may what you want for us come to pass on this tiny earth, obeying the laws of the universe; give us now our daily food, and forgive us for forgetting you, as we will try to forgive those who forget us. We respect your power, as we remain ignorant of your nature, but confident that your plan is loving and inclusive. Amen.*

The Lord's Prayer is not only perfect but of all prayers uttered it is the most popular. It is the only prayer most Christians memorize except perhaps "Now I lay me down to sleep" or the table grace, "God is great and God is good." It is so much a part of us that we use it without thinking. An instructor of public speaking at a Georgia manufacturing plant was asked to give a speech at an annual banquet. He began by suggesting that they all stand and recite the pledge of allegiance. He proudly faced the flag, shoulders squared, hand over heart, and said, "Our Father who art in heaven . . . ."

The prayer's popularity is shown by its constant use by most Christians. Sometimes it is used to teach. Luther said, "I wish that women would recite the Lord's Prayer every time before opening their mouths."

The Lord's Prayer is memorized by little children who use it the rest of their lives. It is heard and prayed in the public worship of all churches, prayed verbally or sung as a solo, anthem, or congregational hymn. Church organizations use it to open and/or close their meetings. Individuals use it for personal prayers, often as a conclusion to their morning and evening prayer.

Dual Biblical Accounts

The two accounts are recorded in Matthew 6:9-13 and Luke 11:1-4. The occasion for Jesus' giving the prayer: Matthew gives the prayer in the Sermon on the Mount when Jesus teaches about prayer. Luke tells how the Disciples saw and heard Jesus praying. They came to him with the request: "Lord, teach us to pray." They apparently felt with Paul who wrote, "We do not know how to pray as we ought" (Romans 8:26). In response to their request Jesus gives them a model prayer for them to "pray like Jesus." He does not give them a lecture on how to pray. He does not discuss the theology of prayer. He teaches by an example which is not to replace their individual prayers but to serve as a model for their own prayers.

The Dual Biblical Accounts

Matthew 6:9-13

"Our Father in heaven, hallowed be your name. Your kingdom come. Your will be done on earth, as it is in heaven. Give us this day our daily bread. And forgive us our debts, as we also have forgiven our debtors. And do not bring us to the time of trial, but rescue us from the evil one."

Luke 11:1-4

"Father, hallowed be your name. Your kingdom come. Give us each day our daily bread. And forgive us our sins, for we ourselves forgive everyone indebted to us. And do not bring us to the time of trial."

The Differences

1. Matthew gives the prayer as a part of Jesus' teaching on prayer; Luke gives the prayer as a response to the Disciples' request how to pray.

2. Matthew uses "debts" whereas Luke uses "sins."

3. Luke omits from the prayer: "our," "in heaven," "Your will be done" and "Deliver us from evil." The church, therefore, uses Matthew's version for worship.

Dual Church Versions

Traditional

Our Father, who art in heaven, hallowed be thy name, thy kingdom come, thy will be done on earth, as it is in heaven. Give us this day our daily bread; and forgive us our trespasses, as we forgive those who trespass against us; and lead us not into temptation, but deliver us from evil. For thine is the kingdom, and the power, and the glory, forever and ever. Amen.

Contemporary

Our Father in heaven, hallowed be your name, your kingdom come, your will be done on earth, as it is in heaven. Give us today our daily bread. Forgive us our sins as we forgive those who sin against us. Save us from the time of trial and deliver us from evil. For the kingdom, the power, and the glory are yours, now and forever. Amen.

The Differences

1. The contemporary version uses "Your" rather than "Thy."

2. The word is "sins" rather than "trespasses."

3. "Temptation" is expressed as "time of trial."

The Church's Addition

The conclusion, "For thine is the kingdom ..." is an addition to the words of Jesus. The concluding words of the prayer are not in the best manuscripts of the New Testament. They were added by the church early in the second century to round out the prayer for use in worship.

The Roman Catholic church does not add the concluding words of praise but stops where Jesus stopped: "Deliver us from evil." Roman Catholics are more faithful to the Scriptures in this case while Protestants follow the tradition of the church. It is usually the opposite.

The church's addition to the Lord's Prayer is based upon Daniel 4:3 — "His kingdom is an everlasting kingdom, and his sovereignty is from generation to generation." A second source comes from David's prayer in 1 Chronicles 29:11 — "Yours, O Lord, are the greatness, the power, the glory, the victory, and the majesty."

Dual Content

Jesus divided his prayer into two main parts concerning humanity's two main concerns. In part A Jesus teaches us to pray about God. There are three petitions characterized by the use of "Thy" or "Your":

1. "Hallowed be *thy* name"
2. "*Thy* kingdom come"
3. "*Thy* will be done"

With Jesus God the Father always came first. So, in this prayer we deal first with God and our responsibilities to him. It is a lesson for us to always put God first in our lives as well as in our prayers.

Part B deals with human needs. The common word used in each petition is "us."

1. "Give *us* ... our daily bread"
2. "Forgive *us*"
3. "Lead *us* not into temptation"
4. "Deliver *us* from evil"

Two Ways To Pray The Lord's Prayer

Pray It By Words

There are certain disadvantages to this type of praying:

1. It is possible to say the words without thinking about what you are saying. Some times a leader will say to a group, "Let us *repeat* the Lord's Prayer." For some that is all it is, just words. Jesus warned against this type of praying, "Do not heap up empty phrases" (Matthew 6:7). It is quite possible to say the words while the mind is on something else.

2. By just saying words, we tend to repeat the words over and over. Medieval monks would pray the Lord's Prayer as many as 500 times to gain merit for salvation. The rosary can be used in the same way: repeated prayers to Mary or Jesus. The Buddhists have a prayer wheel filled with prayers. As the wheel is turned, the prayers are offered. The wheel can be spun to increase the number of prayers offered. Jesus taught that the much saying of words had no effect upon God. It is the thoughts and not the words that get to heaven's ear.

3. The way we say the Lord's Prayer indicates we are thinking of what we are saying. After the words, "Thy will be done," many pause as though it were the end of a thought. Then they continue "on earth as it is in heaven." If we were thinking of what we were saying, we would want his will to be done on earth, not just done. Another indication we are saying only words is in our pronunciation of "trespass" and "trespasses." Usually we pronounce both the same with the accent on the second syllable. We do not indicate the difference between a verb and a noun. "Trespasses" is a noun with accent on the first syllable. "Trespass" is a verb with accent on the second syllable.

There are advantages to praying the Lord's Prayer by words.

1. We are using the very words of Jesus. We are praying a perfect prayer.

2. When we say the words of the prayer, we know we are praying aright. This gives us confidence and assurance that this prayer is heard.

3. By praying the words, we can do it corporately. It is easy for all to pray in unison. This binds us together as though we were one person.

Pray It By Thoughts

What are you thinking about when you say the words? What is going through your mind as you say each petition? Another way to pray the Lord's Prayer is to fashion your own prayer in your own words as you go through the Lord's Prayer.

Words	Thoughts
1. Our Father	1. Confidence, immanence of God
2. Who art in heaven	2. Awe, fear, transcendence of God
3. Hallowed be thy name	3. Reverence
4. Thy kingdom come	4. Hoping, working for the kingdom to come
5. Thy will be done	5. Submission

144

6. Give us this day	6. Gratitude
7. Forgive us	7. Forgiveness
8. Lead us not into temptation	8. Strength to say No
9. Deliver us from evil	9. Courage to face evil
10. Thine is the kingdom	10. Praise
11. Amen	11. Assurance

Thoughts On The Words

Our

It is not "my" personal, individual prayer. It is a prayer for the Christian community. Originally it was given to the 12 Disciples for their use. We are one in our faith in God. We are praying to our God, not the god of another religion. That God is the Father of our Lord Jesus Christ.

Father

The God we pray to is our father. Jesus referred to God as Father 170 times. "Father" is never used in the Old Testament for prayer. Jeremias, a renowned Biblical scholar, writes, "There is not a single example of the use of 'Abba' ... as an address to God in the whole of Jewish literature." "Abba" is an Aramaic word for father, meaning Daddy.

The term, Father, may be offensive to some feminists. The term does not refer to sex but to a role. God is asexual. The role of a father is one who is the progenitor, provider, and protector.

"Father" reflects the immanence of God. He is close, dear, and warm as a good father is to his children. As a father, we can come into his presence with cheerfulness and confidence. As a father, he knows us, he cares for us, and he loves us.

We can call God our Father because we are his children by adoption. In baptism, by grace we became his children. Only baptized Christians can call God father, because by baptism that is who he is and who we are.

Heaven

God is in heaven, high above us. It reminds us of the transcendence of God — the totally other God, invisible, incomprehensible, immortal, omnipotent, and omniscient. That thought causes us to be filled with awe and adoration.

Hallowed

God's name is in itself holy. We pray here that it might be considered holy by us. The name stands for the person of God. It identifies and describes his nature. The name is unpronounceable — YHWH. Scholars added vowels to make it "Yahweh." A substitute name is "Adonai" meaning "Lord."

Thus, we speak and use God's name with reverence. To respect his name is to respect God. It is so important that one of the 10 Commandments is "You shall not take the name of the Lord thy God in vain." There are many serious violations of this in today's culture as expressed in movies, TV, novels, drama, and pornography.

Kingdom Come

God's kingdom is the rule of God. It will come on earth of itself. We cannot bring the Kingdom. We can only hope, pray, and work for its coming. It is a kingdom of love, righteousness, and peace. We pray that the kingdom will come on earth. We hope that the kingdoms of this world will become the Kingdom of God. This is what we live for, work for, and hope for. The Kingdom will be here when "every knee shall bow and every tongue confess that Jesus Christ is Lord" (Philippians 2:10-11).

Thy Will

In Gethsemane Jesus prayed, "Not my will but thine be done." It is a prayer of submission. What is his will? Micah answers: "To do justice, and to love kindness, and to walk humbly with your God" (Micah 6:8). In submitting to God's will, it is helpful to remember that God's will is always good and for our good. Bending our wills to God's will may cause a bloody sweat as happened in Gethsemane.

Daily Bread

God gives us food whether we pray or not just as he sends rain on the godly and ungodly. Here we express gratitude for our daily bread. It refers to the providence of God. He is the author of all we have and are. This petition embraces all of our physical needs, not only our food.

Forgive

When we ask God for forgiveness, we are admitting that we have grieviously sinned in many ways and offended him. We know that if we truly repent and believe, we will be forgiven. That assurance is based upon the grace of God manifest in the cross of Christ.

As We Forgive

This is the most difficult part to pray. We ask God to forgive us as we forgive. We are saying that we want God to treat us as we treat our worst enemy. It means foregoing revenge and retaliation. Here is the catch: We will not be forgiven unless we first forgive. Jesus taught: "If you do not forgive others, neither will your Father forgive your trespasses" (Matthew 6:15).

Temptation

God does not tempt anyone. Jesus wrote, "He himself tempts no one" (James 1:13). The contemporary version of the Lord's Prayer is more accurate: "Save us from the time of trial." To be tempted is to be tested. We pray here that when such trials or tests come, God will give us strength to overcome them. It is praying for strength to say "No" to Satan.

Deliver

Here we pray for courage. We live in a wicked world and are subject to the evils around us. We may be victims of crime. We may endure innocent suffering, injustice, poverty, and racism. We live increasingly in a violent society and we may get hurt. We pray for courage to face the world's worst. We cannot escape the world's tribulations but we can react to the worst by being and doing the best.

Doxology

We conclude the prayer with praise, assurance, and confidence. We confess that God's kingdom is eternal. His Word shall endure. We leave our prayer with confidence that God is and that his will shall be done.

Amen

The final word in the prayer is "Amen." It means verily, truly, it shall be so. It is an affirmation of faith that God has heard our prayer and will answer according to his will.

The following was written by an unknown English soldier during an air raid during World War II. He huddled one night in an air raid shelter and wrote this on the back of a church bulletin.

> *I cannot say "Our" if I live in a watertight compartment.*
> *I cannot say "Father" if I do not demonstrate the relationship in my daily life.*
> *I cannot say "which art in heaven" if I am so occupied with the earth that I am laying up no treasure there.*
> *I cannot say "hallowed be Thy name" if I am not doing all in my power to hasten its coming.*
> *I cannot say "Thy will be done" if I am questioning, resentful of, or disobedient to his will for me.*
> *I cannot say "on earth as it is in heaven" if I am not prepared to devote my life here to his service.*
> *I cannot say "Give us this day our daily bread" if I am living on past experience or if I am an under-the-counter shopper.*
> *I cannot say "Forgive us our trespasses as we forgive those that trespass against us" if I harbor a grudge against anyone.*
> *I cannot say "Lead us not into temptation" if I deliberately place myself in a position to be tempted.*
> *I cannot say "Deliver us from evil" if I am not prepared to fight it in the spiritual realm with the weapon of prayer.*
> *I cannot say "Thine is the power" if I fear what men may do or what my neighbors think.*